ANOTHER CHANCE

LAWRENCE MAXWELL

Pacific Press Publishing Association
Boise, Idaho
Oshawa, Ontario, Canada

Edited by B. Russell Holt
Designed by Tim Larson
Cover photos by Betty Blue
Typeset in 10/12 Century Schoolbook

Unless otherwise noted, all Scripture quotations are from the New International Version.

Library of Congress Cataloging-in-Publication Data:

Maxwell, Lawrence.
   Another chance / Lawrence Maxwell.
        p.   cm.
   ISBN 0-8163-1165-X
   1. Bible. O.T. Ezra—Criticism, interpretation, etc. 2. Bible. O.T. Nehemiah—Criticism, Interpretation, etc. 3. Bible. O.T. Ezra—Study and teaching. 4. Bible. O.T. Nehemiah—Study and teaching. I. Title.
   BS1355.2.M388 1993
   222'.706—dc20
                                       93-1415
                                          CIP

93 94 95 96 97 ● 5 4 3 2 1

Contents

Chapter 1
Why Study Ezra and Nehemiah?

"Go and tell it to the world."

"No, Lord. You know I cannot preach."

"Start out, and I will help you."

"No, Lord. Besides, Lord, I may be wrong. Perhaps my figures aren't correct. I don't want to mislead people."

For thirteen years the old farmer had refused to tell what he had discovered in the Bible. For thirteen years, the Lord had insisted that he should tell everyone.

Now, on this Saturday morning, the Lord was being particularly persistent, and the old farmer, just as adamant. But God did not intend to be disobeyed anymore. The farmer's figures were close enough, and his message must go out.

Finally the old farmer got out of his chair, slipped to his knees, and leaned his form reverently against the desk where he had studied the Bible so diligently these past one and a half decades. A pleased smile creased his weathered face. He had thought of a way to agree to do what the Lord was asking without actually doing it.

"Lord," he prayed, "Thou knowest I cannot preach. But I will, if someone comes to invite me."

He sat back in his chair, relaxed. He knew no one would ask a fifty-year-old farmer to preach a sermon in a church on a Sunday morning. He had nothing more to worry about.

The story has been told so many times—I am sure it is familiar to every reader of this book—how within half an hour of that prayer a loud knocking on the farmhouse door announced the presence of the farmer's nephew, Irving, who said that he'd been riding horseback since before breakfast. "The minister who was supposed to preach at the Baptist church tomorrow can't be there," he said. "Dad sent me to ask if you'd come, Uncle William, and tell us what you've been learning in the Bible about the second coming of the Lord."

Just what he had been so sure would never happen!

Without a word to his nephew, William Miller—for he, of course, was the old farmer—turned on his heel, jerked open the back door, and strode angrily across the lawn to a grove of maple trees, where he had frequently prayed before. He was angry with God for what He was asking him to do, angry with himself for the promise he had made, and dreadfully afraid. For an hour he wrestled, like Jacob, till he finally gave in and agreed to keep his promise. He would go preach for his nephew's father. Such relief flooded his soul that he skipped and hopped, jumping up and down and praising the Lord, quite frightening his little daughter Lucy, who ran into the house calling, "Mommy, come quick! Daddy's going crazy."

After lunch, Miller rode with his nephew the sixteen miles to Dresden on the extra horse Irving had brought with him. On Sunday morning, in his sister's kitchen, he gave his very first sermon. The congregation was so enthusiastic, they asked for more. Miller gave them a series that lasted most of the week, probably transferring the meetings to the church, which was packed with eager listeners before the week was over.

And when Miller returned home, there was another invitation to preach, and soon after that another and another—and the rest is history.

But what does all this have to do with our study of Ezra and Nehemiah?

A very great deal, indeed!

Because William Miller's preaching was the cradle from which the Seventh-day Adventist Church has grown.

Our message that Christ is coming soon is based on his study of the great prophecy of the 2,300 days.

Our unique teaching that Christ is at this very time—even as we speak—in the heavenly sanctuary blotting out the sins of the faithful is all tied in with Miller's preaching of the 2,300 days.

Our confidence that we should at this time be preaching the

messages of the three angels of Revelation 14:6-12 is an outgrowth of that same 2,300-day prophecy that Miller had been so reluctant to tell anyone about.

And while the prophecy itself appears in Daniel, we wouldn't know when in history it began to be fulfilled except that the date is given by Ezra. And Ezra's compatriot Nehemiah gave substance to the decree that Ezra received from King Artaxerxes and that marks the beginning of the great prophecy.

It is, therefore, because of Ezra and Nehemiah that we know that the 2,300-day prophecy ended in 1844. Because of Ezra and Nehemiah, we know that Christ's work in the Most Holy Place is going on *now*. Because of Ezra and Nehemiah, we know that we *ought* to be preaching the three angels' messages. Because of them, we know that our church, the Seventh-day Adventist Church, is God's church for these last days. It is His church for *us*.

With so much growing out of these two books, obviously it will be worth our while to study them.

But this is not all.

How God treats sinners

Although, as we shall find, these two books recount a great many interesting things about the Jews and their leaders, the fundamental reason why God has protected them over the years is that we may learn what they tell us about God.

This is true of every book in the Bible. The Bible was written to tell us about God—His greatness and power on the one hand, and His gracious lovingkindness on the other. For instance, Samson's life and death are not recorded in the Bible to impress us that a man could catch three hundred foxes and attach firebrands to their tails or that he could kill one thousand Philistines with the jawbone of a dead donkey or that he could lift a city's gates and carry them for miles on his back. What is much more important, and wonderfully encouraging, is to understand that Samson could not have done any of these amazing feats without God's help, including pulling down the Philistine temple. The great reason Samson's life is recorded in the Bible is to prove that when a sinner repents, God is willing to take him back and give him another chance, even when he sins and repents again and again.

So, in the study of Ezra and Nehemiah, let us remember that these books were not preserved all these years to tell us how many people went back to Jerusalem under Zerubbabel or that the citizens under Nehemiah rebuilt Jerusalem's walls in fifty-two days, important as these items are. These books were written to tell us about God.

Let's be alert all the way through to catch these revelations.

Where in time are Ezra and Nehemiah?

I think one reason so many people—even some Adventists—don't understand the Bible better is that they are confused about when things happened.

Ezra and Nehemiah can suffer particularly from this problem, because their books are not located in the Bible where they might be expected. A quick glance in the Bible shows that the books of Ezra and Nehemiah come long before those of Daniel, Haggai, and Zechariah, which are located near the end of the Old Testament, although all these men lived much closer together in time than the placement of their books would suggest. It is so very easy to be confused about this! One can't really do justice to these two great leaders, Ezra and Nehemiah, without recognizing the important contributions Daniel and Haggai and Zechariah made to the success of their work.

Put them on a chart!

Here's a chart to help solve this serious problem. I find charts helpful in situations like these. I'll let you help me develop this one, because I have trouble understanding fully developed charts. I'd much rather watch someone putting in the details and explaining as he goes along.

First, draw a line to represent history from Creation to the present:

Put a date on each end:

|—————————————————————————————|

4000 B.C.   A.D. 2000

Draw two vertical lines that divide the long line into three equal parts:

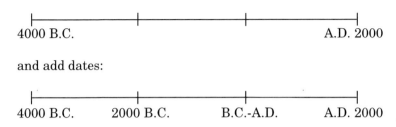

4000 B.C.   A.D. 2000

and add dates:

4000 B.C.   2000 B.C.   B.C.-A.D.   A.D. 2000

When we put names on these dates, we make a most interesting discovery:

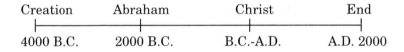

Creation	Abraham	Christ	End
4000 B.C.	2000 B.C.	B.C.-A.D.	A.D. 2000

Almost exactly two thousand years lay between Creation and Abraham, two thousand years between Abraham and Christ, and two thousand years between Christ and us. This means that God gave one-third of history to the people before Abraham, one-third to the Jews, and one-third to the Christians. I don't know how much significance we should draw from this, but I find it highly intriguing that the three periods are so nearly the same length.

Now let's draw a vertical line through the middle:

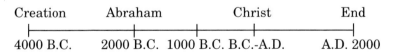

Creation	Abraham		Christ	End
4000 B.C.	2000 B.C.	1000 B.C.	B.C.-A.D.	A.D. 2000

That central line, which is, of course, 1000 B.C., marks the high point in the reign of King David. David came to the throne in 1011 B.C. and reigned until 971 B.C. (see *SDA Bible Commentary,* vol. 2, p. 77). This means that David's encounter with Goliath, his trials in the cave of Adullam, and his heartfelt repentance for his sin with Bathsheba all occurred almost exactly on the midpoint between creation and the second coming. I confess I felt a tingle of excitement when I discovered that. And, by the way, this is no rough estimate. These dates are considered to be correct to within just a year or two.

As for the criticism by some non-Christians that Bible stories are myths of "once upon a time" in a "never-never land," consider this. David was thirty years old when he came to the throne and was (probably) seventeen when he felled Goliath. We can add thirteen years (30-17=13) to 1011 B.C. and say that his famous encounter with the giant took place beside a brook a few miles from Bethlehem in the spring of 1034 B.C.—and be sure we are right within a year or two and a mile or two! Myths cannot be dated or located like that. There isn't room on our small chart to print *David and Goliath* in its proper place. Perhaps you can pencil it in with tiny letters.

But what about Ezra and Nehemiah?

With these major historical landmarks established, we are well on our way to finding where Ezra and Nehemiah fit. Their dates are firmly established, as we shall see later. Ezra made his first trip to Jerusalem in 457 B.C., and Nehemiah first went there in 444 B.C. This puts them between the middle line and the B.C.-A.D. line on our chart; actually, just past the center of this period, at the location of the star:

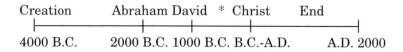

These were men with a mission. Let's put on our chart the events that made their work so important—and so necessary. Since we have so little space, let's concentrate on the thousand-year period between David and Christ:

The period began with much hope and optimism. David was everybody's favorite king. At this time, before Absalom's rebellion,

David was riding high. "Whatsoever the king did pleased all the people" (2 Samuel 3:36, KJV). Both David and his son Solomon reigned over all Israel. This period is known as the time of the united kingdom.

When Solomon's son, Rehoboam, came to the throne, he made a brief speech that he thought would confirm his power, glory, and wisdom for ever. In fact, it proved him to be immature and foolish (see 1 Kings 12:1-19). It spawned most of the difficulties Ezra and Nehemiah encountered half a millennium later, and its long-range effects even gave Jesus problems. Its immediate effect was to split the kingdom instantly. Ten tribes pulled out the same day, crowned their own king, and established their own capital. From then on, these ten tribes are known as the kingdom of Israel or the northern kingdom. They eventually built a new capital on a hilltop vineyard thirty-five miles north of Jerusalem and called it Samaria. Remember that city Samaria. It's going to cause Ezra and Nehemiah many, many problems.

Rehoboam, Solomon's son, was left with two tribes known as the kingdom of Judah or the southern kingdom. Its capital was the ancient city of Jerusalem.

This dividing of the kingdom came about in 931 B.C. We'll put it on the chart.

David   Jesus
    931 B.C.

1000 B.C.   B.C.-A.D.

From the beginning, the northern kingdom was in rebellion not only against the southern kingdom but also against God. One of the first acts of Jeroboam, the king of the new northern kingdom, was to provide two golden calves, one in Bethel near Jerusalem and the other at Dan in the far north, so the people would go to them to worship and not to the temple in Jerusalem. One bad king followed another. Finally God let an Assyrian army enter Samaria and take all its ten tribes captive. This was in 722 B.C.

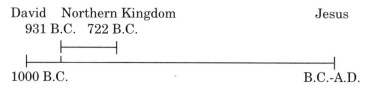

The Assyrians attempted to repopulate the area by bringing in people from other nations. But apparently not enough came, for wild animals increased to the point that they threatened the lives of the new inhabitants. Being heathen and believing that each territory had its own gods, the newcomers appealed to the Assyrian emperor to send some Israelites back to teach them how to please the gods of the land, thinking that then the gods would help control the wild beasts. The emperor was agreeable and brought back some Israelites. They intermarried with the pagans, and the resulting peoples, with their mixed religion, became known as Samaritans.

Meanwhile, the southern kingdom also had some bad kings, such as Asa and Manasseh, as well as several good ones, such as Hezekiah and Josiah. But eventually the bad outweighed the good, and God let the Babylonians under Nebuchadnezzar destroy Jerusalem and take the kingdom of Judah into exile. This is the famous Babylonian exile. It began in 605 B.C., though Jerusalem was not fully destroyed until 586 B.C. Mark 605 B.C. on the chart:

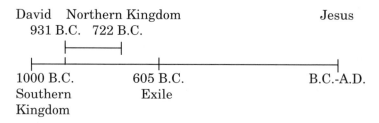

The Babylonian exile lasted seventy years. With permission from the Persian emperor, Cyrus, the Jews began to return to Jerusalem in 536 B.C. (If that seems like only sixty-nine years, remember that the Jews counted *inclusively;* if something started Monday afternoon and ended Wednesday morning they said it lasted three days.) Add 536 B.C.:

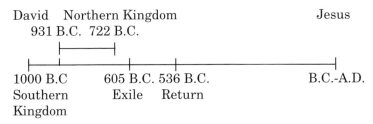

The returnees ran into a great deal of trouble, especially from the Samaritans. After a while God raised up Haggai and Zechariah to help them. These two men worked in Jerusalem during 520-515 B.C. Our chart is getting crowded, so we'll label them H&Z:

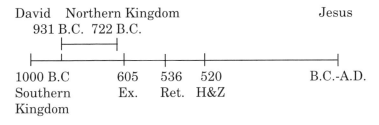

Ezra begins his book with an account of the return in 536 B.C. He tells about the decree of Cyrus, which made the return possible, and lists the heads of all the families that went at that time. Ezra himself went to Jerusalem in 457 B.C. with a decree from Artaxerxes, soon to be followed by Nehemiah in 444 B.C. Let's put in the dates for these men. To give ourselves room, we'll let the whole line represent the time from the return in 536 B.C. up to the preaching of Malachi, which ended the Old Testament about 400 B.C.

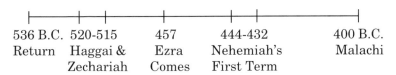

Now we can see that Haggai and Zechariah actually lived and worked *before* Ezra and Nehemiah, even though their books come later in the Bible! Why are their books placed where they are?

There is a simple explanation.

In ancient times, the Old Testament was divided into three sections—history, poetry, and prophets. Genesis through Esther are history books, arranged very much in chronological order. Job through Song of Solomon are poetry. Isaiah through Malachi are the books of the prophets. Ezra and Nehemiah, being late in Old Testament history, belong correctly near the end of the history series, even though this puts them before the psalms. Haggai and Zechariah, almost the last of the prophets, correctly belong near the end of the prophet section. Malachi, by the way, may have worked in Jerusalem during Nehemiah's second term. If not, he came along soon afterward.

In studying the books of Ezra and Nehemiah, with some help from the books of Esther, Malachi, Haggai, Zechariah, and the closing chapters of Daniel, we will follow God's dealings with His wayward people from 536 to 400 B.C., a period of only 136 years. Short in time, these years are long on evidences of God's care, the damaging effects of disobedience, and the amazing feats ordinary people can do when they consecrate themselves to God.

Ezra 1, 2

Chapter 2
Another Chance!

Another chance! How much we all want one, no matter how many we've been given before. Again and again we mess things up and wish we might start over. And the great and powerful God, who has every right to be offended by our sinfulness, graciously gives us chance after chance after chance.

This glorious truth is one of the outstanding messages of Ezra-Nehemiah. If you're bored by the frequent lists of names, bewildered by so many kings, or confused by all the enemies who opposed the exiles' return, simply grasp this one sublime assurance—another chance!—and your study of these two books will have been well worth all the time you put into it.

Slaves longing to breathe free
When the book of Ezra opens, God's people are exiles, ruled by idol worshipers because of the high-handed way they have rejected God's rulership. The last verses of 2 Chronicles summarize the situation as it was at the beginning of the exile. Compressing three hundred years into a few sentences, the author wrote:

> All the leaders of the priests and the people became more and more unfaithful, following all the detestable practices of the nations and defiling the temple of the Lord, which he had consecrated in Jerusalem.
> The Lord, the God of their fathers, sent word to them through his messengers again and again, because he had pity on his people and on his dwelling place. But

15

they mocked God's messengers, despised his words and scoffed at his prophets until the wrath of the Lord was aroused against his people and there was no remedy. He brought up against them the king of the Babylonians, who killed their young men with the sword in the sanctuary, and spared neither young man nor young woman, old man or aged. God handed all of them over to Nebuchadnezzar. He carried to Babylon all the articles from the temple of God, both large and small, and the treasures of the Lord's temple and the treasures of the king and his officials. They set fire to God's temple and broke down the wall of Jerusalem; they burned all the palaces and destroyed everything of value there.

He carried into exile to Babylon the remnant, who escaped from the sword, and they became servants to him and his sons (2 Chronicles 36:14-20).

Chance after chance after chance

In spite of all God's blessings, His people had let Him down. Yet God would give them another chance. That's one of the most wonderful things about our God. He had done it before many times. After Adam and Eve disobeyed, God gave them another chance outside the garden. When the antediluvians failed, God gave Noah and his family the wonderful chance of starting over. When Noah's descendants apostatized, God gave Abraham the chance to be father of His chosen people. When, in Egypt, Abraham's grand-children absorbed the ways of the heathen, God brought them out and personally instructed them in the lifestyle He wanted them to follow.

And when, on the border of the Promised Land, Moses warned the Israelites that if they disobeyed, exile would be the sure result, he also told them of God's offer to bring them home and give them yet another chance if they would repent and return to Him:

When you and your children return to the Lord your God and obey him with all your heart and with all your soul according to everything I command you today, then the Lord your God will restore your fortunes and have compassion on you and gather you again from all the nations where he scattered you. Even if you have been banished to the most distant land under the heavens, from there the Lord your God will gather you and bring you back (Deuteronomy 30:2-4).

How many times the exiled Jews must have encouraged themselves with that prophecy while they languished in Babylon, yearning to breathe free again!

And there was another promise God had made, especially for them. It predicted the exact length of their exile.

The seventy years

A few months after Nebuchadnezzar took the first group of captives to Babylon (including Daniel), God sent Jeremiah to tell the citizens of Jerusalem, "It shall come to pass, when seventy years are accomplished, that I will punish the king of Babylon, and that nation, saith the Lord, for their iniquity, and the land of the Chaldeans, and will make it perpetual desolations" (Jeremiah 25:12, KJV). How kind of God to encourage them that way!

Eight years after that group was taken, the Babylonian army returned to Jerusalem and took another group, this time including Ezekiel. Jeremiah wrote the captives a letter reminding them of God's promise: "After seventy years be accomplished at Babylon I will visit you, and perform my good word toward you, in causing you to return to this place" (Jeremiah 29:10, KJV).

Daniel's problem

As one of the first captives, Daniel, we can be sure, began counting the seventy years with 605 B.C., the year he was taken to Babylon. One can almost hear his countdown as the years went by: "Seventy, sixty-nine, sixty-eight . . . forty-five, forty-four, forty-three . . . seventeen, sixteen . . . only fifteen more years till deliverance day!"

Why, then, does he tell us in Daniel 9:1, 2: "In the first year of Darius . . . , I Daniel understood by books the number of the years, whereof the word of the Lord came to Jeremiah the prophet, that he would accomplish seventy years in the desolations of Jerusalem" (KJV)? He was around eighty-five years old by this time. Babylon had fallen and Darius the Mede[1] had taken the throne. The exile had lasted some sixty-eight years. Why does Daniel make such a careful study *then*? Why is his study followed by such an anguished prayer for God to fulfill what He had so clearly promised?

Daniel's problem can be found in the words of Gabriel in Daniel 8:14. He knew that the first thing the exiles would do when they reached Jerusalem would be to rebuild the temple and get all the sacred services going, including cleansing the sanctuary on the Day of Atonement. But Gabriel said: "Unto two thousand and three hundred days; then shall the sanctuary be cleansed" (KJV). Just when Daniel thought the seventy years were nearly over, Gabriel had come with this message that seemed to extend the return into the far-distant future. The implications were so discouraging that Daniel was sick for several days (see Daniel 8:27).

2,300 years, not days

From the beginning of the Adventist Church, Adventists have taken the position that the 2,300 days refer to 2,300 *years*. Many non-Adventist Bible commentators interpret them as simply 2,300 literal days, then apply them to a second-rate politician whose friends may have burned a pig on the temple altar in 168 B.C.

These people would do well to give a closer look at Daniel 8:27. Here is some of the finest biblical proof that the 2,300 days are actually 2,300 years. It is presented so unconsciously that it is all the more impressive. It was not written to settle an argument; it simply describes how Daniel felt. But it surely puts the argument to rest!

At the time Daniel saw the 2,300-day vision, he thought that only fifteen of the seventy years remained.[2] If the 2,300 days were in fact only 2,300 literal days, when he came out of the vision, he would have raced through the house looking for his wife, shouting, "Honey, honey! It's going to be only another six and a half years till the temple is restored!"

Of course, since he didn't have a wife, he couldn't have done that. But at least we ought to see him racing out to the royal stables, calling to his favorite driver to hitch the swiftest horses to the fastest chariot. "We've got to get down to the river Chebar, quick!" he explains to the startled horseman. "Oh, but Ezekiel is going to be excited when he hears this! Only six and a half years! Think of it! That's less than half the time I figured till deliverance. But the angel told me just now that the temple will be built and the services conducted and the Day of Atonement fully observed only six and a half years from now. Praise the Lord!"

What we actually see is nothing of the sort. Daniel says he was so overwhelmed with perplexity and disappointment he took to his bed (see Daniel 8:27, KJV). The only way to explain this is that Daniel knew the angel was talking about 2,300 *years*.[3]

Crushing disappointment

As we have noticed, Daniel had been looking forward eagerly to the captives' return. With only fifteen years remaining, he might actually live to see it! Then here came this dreadful message. The restoration of the temple had been put off 2,300 years. The angel had emphasized the long length of the time. "The vision . . . shall be for many days," he had said (Daniel 8:26, KJV). What a terrible, terrible disappointment.

Daniel got out his records and studied them as he had never studied them before. He may have had to make extensive inquiries and long trips to distant synagogues in order to find copies of Jeremiah's writings. He certainly didn't have the convenient Bible we have, where he could read the various prophecies by flipping a few pages.

Searching for Isaiah

At first, with his discouraged outlook, he may have admitted that the seventy years just might have started later. Maybe he had been too hopeful all along. We can see him putting the scrolls away and returning to the king's business and waiting, still counting the years but not so hopefully now. And then, from his advantaged position close to the seat of government, he hears of a Persian named Cyrus who is challenging the Babylonian armies and winning victories over them. The name strikes a chord in his memory. Didn't Isaiah write something about a Cyrus who would send God's people home?

See Daniel on his next business trip talking to the local rabbi after the Sabbath service—maybe at the large synagogue by the river Chebar, asking the rabbi to help him locate the passage where Isaiah said something about a man named Cyrus sending the exiles home. (Tradition credits Ezekiel with originating the idea of synagogues, and he lived by the river Chebar. The Jews are known to have started worshiping in synagogues during the Babylonian exile, since they could not go to the temple in Jerusalem. The buildings usually had a special cupboard for preserving whatever Scripture scrolls the synagogue owned. So this trip on which we have sent Daniel may not be so totally imaginary!)

Daniel was still studying when Darius took the kingdom in 539 B.C. The timing of the event fit Jeremiah's seventy years perfectly. Cyrus was Darius the Mede's superior officer, but he chose to wait a while before proclaiming himself the new emperor of a new empire. Daniel knew the event would have to take place soon; then everything would be set to fulfill Isaiah's prophecy.

Why the delay?

By this time there is absolutely no doubt in Daniel's mind. That's what he tells us in Daniel 9:1, 2. The captivity was to last seventy years, just as he'd thought. But why this 2,300-year delay?

Only sin could bring a delay like this, and the Jews had sinned. Ezekiel had told Daniel the awful things he had been shown in vision—things that were going on in the temple long after the second captives came to Babylon (see Ezekiel 8). And certainly Daniel himself had seen many Jews in Babylon who made no profession of the old faith. God certainly had reason for delaying His promise. "But no, it must not be," Daniel says to himself. "God is forgiving. God is merciful." And God had said, "Ye shall seek me, and find me, when ye shall search for me with all your heart" (Jeremiah 29:13, KJV).

The old man sinks to his knees. From the depths of his breaking heart, great, swelling cries rise to heaven: "O Lord, listen! O Lord, forgive! O Lord, hear and act! For your sake, O my God, *do not delay*, because your city and your people bear your Name" (Daniel 9:19, emphasis supplied).

At that point Daniel felt a hand on his shoulder. Gabriel had come to comfort him, to assure him that the 2,300-day prophecy would not delay the return of the exiles. Daniel smiled through his tears. The exiles would return on time.

But first, the lions' den

Whether the night with the lions came before Daniel's prayer or after, we are not told. But it is a warning to all of us not to pray for something we are unwilling to pay a price for. You see, Daniel's night in the lions' den had much to do with getting the exiles home on time, the thing he had so earnestly prayed for. Daniel's faith even in a den of lions impressed Cyrus that here was a man he must listen to (see *Prophets and Kings,* p. 557). And Cyrus's reaction helped answer the questions Daniel must have asked on the way to the den, "Why me? Why now?"

When Daniel finished showing Cyrus what the Hebrew prophets had written so many years before, the ruler willingly agreed to let the captives go. He even went beyond granting permission and provided money and other gifts.[4]

Why no time this time?

We often hear it said that God ought to have told us how much time must pass before the second coming as He told the exiles how long it would be until the return to Jerusalem. Surely more people would be ready if they knew exactly how much time was left.

God has responded to this suggestion with three examples.

1. Before the Flood He did announce there would be exactly 120 years to get ready (see Genesis 6:3). He allowed the people to live any lifestyle they chose. Absolutely none of them were prepared when the Flood came except the eight in Noah's immediate family.

2. Before the Exodus He announced there would be 430 years before the trip to Canaan.[5] As deliverance day approached, He allowed the people to suffer painful, humiliating slavery. The result? Everyone left at the appointed time. But so few were ready for life in the Promised Land that God had to let almost every one of them die in the wilderness.

3. During the Babylonian exile He promised to open a way to return to Jerusalem in seventy years and then allowed the exiles to live in comparative comfort. Result? A small percentage of the

exiles took advantage of the opportunity when it came. The majority remained where they were. Of those who went, many were unprepared to live the lifestyle God wanted.

Frankly, it doesn't look as if announcing an exact time helps people get ready. In our contemporary situation, those who will leave the earth at the second coming must be Christ-like. There is no provision for shipping back to earth anyone who makes trouble in heaven. Apparently, the date for the trip to the New Jerusalem depends to a large degree upon the willingness of God's people to cooperate with Him in perfecting their characters.[6] God has good reason for thinking this challenge will be more effective than for Him to set a specific time.

The exile over at last!

News of Cyrus's decree galloped through the empire with the speed of Persia's fastest horses (see Esther 8:10) and stirred up excitement in every Jewish community. The exile was over at last! Many began at once preparing to leave. For a few, no doubt, getting ready was merely a matter of finalizing their preparations; trusting God's promise, they had begun to prepare long ago.

But to many the news came with a jolt. They'd have to face a decision they'd hoped to avoid. They were comfortable in Babylon, with homes and gardens and successful businesses. Did they really want to start over among ruins? The returnees would need money to rebuild. For some it was a question of their children's education; schools here were much better than anything they could hope for in Judea for many years, and by then the children would be grown. Some, no doubt, had friends they hated to leave. And some had married Babylonians; the relatives objected to their going.

But there was great joy among those to whom the news came as a message straight from heaven. Homes were sold, businesses closed, notices given to employers, necessary items purchased, food and clothing packed. Some, like Daniel, who were too old for the long journey, threw their energies into helping those who could. Even the neighbors helped. They "assisted them with articles of silver and gold, with goods and livestock, and with valuable gifts, in addition to all the freewill offerings" (Ezra 1:6).

Even Cyrus helped. "King Cyrus brought out the articles belonging to the temple of the Lord, which Nebuchadnezzar had carried away from Jerusalem," and entrusted them to Zerubbabel, "the prince of Judah" (verses 7, 8), whom he had appointed leader.[7]

Home!

Finally the returnees were on their way, nearly fifty thousand men, women, and children, with more than seven thousand donkeys, horses, camels, and mules to carry their stuff. Do you see Daniel on that long-awaited morning waving them off? I'm sure he was there, wishing he were younger so he could go with them.

The direct route from Babylon to Jerusalem was a bit more than five hundred miles, but hardly anyone went that way, because the land was desert. A group this size had no choice but to take a much longer route northwest along fertile land watered by the Tigris and Euphrates rivers, then follow other waterways west and south till they reached the springs and brooks of Judea.

What a happy group of travelers they were! The many weeks on the road gave plenty of opportunity to explain to the children just why they were walking so far. It was a time to recall the many failures of Israel that had led up to the long years of exile. But now the exile was over. They were on their way home.

And so at last they were there! The burned, weed-covered stones of once-beautiful Jerusalem must have been a disappointment to the youth, who probably asked with some contempt why they had come so far to see *this*! But to the older ones it was home!

The group gathered around the destroyed temple, trying to find space to stand among the toppled stones. They sang psalms, praising God for bringing them safely so far. They prayed, thanking Him that at last they were home. The leaders announced plans for clearing the temple area, beginning with the altar, so that sacrifices could be offered again soon. Zerubbabel, the leader, and Jeshua, the high priest, were hoping to begin services before the Feast of Tabernacles if possible.

And they took up an offering. "Some of the heads of the families gave freewill offerings toward the rebuilding of the house of God on its site" (Ezra 2:68).

Then they separated, going to find the old homesites and make them livable again. But every heart beat with a high and holy resolve. Their parents had sinned, and God had sent them into exile. Now He was giving them, the children, another chance. They intended that their generation would not let Him down.

---

1. Darius the Mede lived about a year after his armies broke into Babylon on the night Belshazzar saw the writing on the wall. Don't confuse him with the emperor Darius who reigned later, while the new temple was being built.

2. Thirteen years passed between Daniel 8 and Daniel 9. Daniel 8 is dated in 551 B.C.; Daniel 9 is 538 B.C. See C. Mervyn Maxwell, *God Cares,* vol. 1, p. 195.

3. That Daniel's study of the books was prompted by his desire to understand the effect the 2,300 days had on the seventy years is clearly stated in *Prophets and Kings,* pages 554, 555: "He could not understand the relation sustained by the seventy years' captivity, as foretold through Jeremiah, to the twenty-three hundred years that in vision he heard the heavenly visitant declare should elapse before the cleansing of God's Sanctuary. . . . Daniel pleaded with the Lord for the speedy fulfillment of these promises." Ellen White, of course, always believed the 2,300 days were 2,300 years. I have pictured Daniel's behavior as I have in order to support Ellen White's interpretation, which I endorse.

4. The financial aid that Cyrus promised is not mentioned in the decree presented in Ezra 1:2-4, but it is mentioned in Ezra 6:3-5. Apparently one edition was for public circulation and the other for officials only.

5. Exodus 12:40, 41 has 430 years. Genesis 15:13 speaks of 400 years. For an explanation, see *Patriarchs and Prophets,* p. 759, note 3.

6. See 2 Peter 3:9 and *Christ's Object Lessons,* p. 69.

7. Sheshbazzar (as he is called in the NIV) is usually referred to by his other name, Zerubbabel.

Chapter 3
Off to a Good Start

The returnees probably never felt closer to one another than when they gathered again in Jerusalem a few weeks after their arrival. They had so many experiences to talk about.

All had found their old homes in some state of disrepair, some completely demolished; we can be sure they wanted to talk about that. Their gardens, after so many years of neglect, had grown up with briars and thorns. There was so much to do, just making things livable again. They wanted to talk about that.

Most of the returnees, having been born in Babylon, had never seen the old family home; they knew of it only from parental descriptions. How did they go about locating their property and proving their claim?

Title to property in those days was protected by written deeds. Normally executed in duplicate, these deeds were written on parchment and signed by several witnesses. One copy was sealed, the other left open. Both were preserved in clay jars.[1] The Bible doesn't say how the exiles managed to protect their deeds when so much around was damaged and destroyed, or how the returnees proved their rights when their deeds were lost. We can be sure, when they came together in Jerusalem, they wanted to talk about that!

And what did they do when they found someone living on their property? How widespread this problem was, we aren't told, but Jeremiah records that after making almost everyone a prisoner of war and methodically destroying Jerusalem, Nebuchadnezzar's chief officer had given the better farms to the poorest people in the land, those he considered not worth taking captive (see Jeremiah 39:10). True, most of these poor people soon moved to Egypt (see Jeremiah 43:5, 7), but did all go? Some must have remained behind. The Samaritans must have envied the better properties and, in the long-continued absence of their owners, moved onto them. By now, these squatters would consider the properties their own. How did the returnees remove them? They'd surely want to talk about *that*!

First things first

But the principal reason they came together as the shadows lengthened under the bright sun of that first autumn of their return was to make sure their relationship with God was so firm and secure that neither they nor their children would ever turn from Him again.

They found that workmen had been busy clearing the temple area and had rebuilt the altar on the very same base where it had always stood. They had come to dedicate that altar and to join in reestablishing the sacrificial service. True, with the temple still in ruins, they could not observe the annual Day of Atonement, which would normally be only ten days away. But at least they had the altar now, and they meant to use it exactly the way Moses had prescribed.

On the first day of Tishri, the seventh month, they gathered reverently as the priest prepared to offer the first sacrifice.

Salvation then and now

With what interest the returnees must have watched on that autumn morning in 536 B.C.! A few of the older persons remembered seeing the service in their childhood; the others had never observed it before. Bowing reverently as the smoke rose above the altar, they reached out by faith to the Saviour represented by the sacrificed lamb; but how dimly they must have pictured Him. Five hundred years and more would pass before men and women could see Him face to face. We are so much more richly favored than they!

But God saved sinners then the same as He does now. Many modern Christians seem to have the concept that God saves sinners differently now from the way He used to. Under Old Testament rules, it is said, sinners were forgiven only when they brought a lamb to the temple, whereas now they are saved by faith alone. But the sacrifice the returnees watched that morning proves this concept false.

No sacrifice had been offered since the destruction of the old temple in 586 B.C. From then till 536 B.C.—fifty years—not one animal had been slain for anyone's sins. Are we to believe that no one found forgiveness during that time? Of course not. Our loving God, who never changes, forgave sinners then the same as He does now, when they placed their faith in His Son, the Lamb of God. It doesn't matter whether we are in exile in Babylon or at home in Jerusalem, He still loves and forgives in response to the prayer of faith.

United in obedience

There was a wonderful feeling of unity in the group. Ezra 3:1 says they were "as one man." What united them was their desire to do everything just the way God had asked. So they remained together for three weeks, till they had observed the week-long Feast of Tabernacles, which began on the fifteenth day of the month. That's a remarkable thing in itself, when you stop to think of it. Winter was coming on, and so many things still needed to be done to their homes before bad weather set in that they could have thought of a thousand excuses for not attending. "A whole week? Man! You must be joking. We've got to get our homes fixed. Heaven helps those who help themselves, you know." They might have said that, but they didn't, because they wanted to do everything right. No more long years in exile for this group!

Twice a day they assembled for the morning and evening sacrifice, and the priests offered all the other sacrifices as well, "in accordance with what is written in the Law of Moses the man of God" (Ezra 3:2).

And God did bless them. Zerubbabel and Jeshua were able to report that already they had hired stone masons and carpenters to do preliminary work on the new temple and had let out contracts to Tyre for cedar trees to be cut and the wood floated down along the Mediterranean coast to Joppa. There was a good chance the temple's foundation could be laid in six or seven months, as soon as good weather returned.

Everyone went to their homes happy and content. This new chance God had given His people was really going well.

The temple begun

Everything was still going well when they gathered again in Jerusalem in the spring of the new year. There was that happy optimism that always comes with the bursting of new leaves and the awakening of spring flowers, when "the cooing of doves is heard in our land" (Song of Solomon 2:12) and the heart sings again with the birds.

This was a very special gathering. The returnees were coming together to dedicate the temple's new foundation. The building that was at the heart and center of everything they held most dear would no longer be in ruins. Here was the clearest evidence imaginable that God was no longer angry with Israel for the sins of the fathers. He had accepted the repentance of the children and had consented to live with them again. "Let them make me a sanctuary; that I may dwell among them," He had said to Moses (Exodus 25:8, KJV). Now He was helping them build another sanctuary; He wanted to be close to them again.

At the appropriate moment, the priests, dressed in their holy garments, blew on their trumpets, the Levites crashed their cymbals, and the choirs answered in paeans of joy, "praising and giving thanks unto the Lord; because he is good, for his mercy endureth for ever toward Israel" (Ezra 3:11, KJV).

As the music rose to its climax, the happy people could contain themselves no longer. Spontaneously they exploded in loud shouts of joy and thanksgiving.

A strange sound

But right then a strange sound was heard, totally unexpected by the younger celebrants. In that day of inexpressible joy, some in the group were actually wailing. Not in repentance of sins they had committed in Jerusalem before the captivity—which would have been appropriate—but in proud contempt of the new temple. "What a pitifully poor little building this is going to be," we hear them exclaim. "In our day, the temple was so much better." They worked themselves up to quite a frenzy, it seems, shouting louder and louder. To drown their disparaging criticisms, the celebrants raised their voices too, till it was impossible to distinguish between the rejoicing and the weeping, and the "noise was heard afar off" (verse 13, KJV).

When people looked to see who was wailing, they saw it was the old men, those who had seen Solomon's temple in its glory, men of sixty and seventy and eighty years, the men who should have been the backbone of this new movement, the ones who should have been first to encourage and strengthen the young. What a dreadful sin older church members commit when they discourage the youth and the young parents in our churches! Who knows how many will be lost to eternity who might have been saved in the kingdom if only one of the older members had given a word of sympathy, a smile of encouragement, a pat on the back, instead of finding fault and criticizing?

The program of dedication was over. The celebrants went home. They were still determined to be faithful. They were still sure God would bless. But something had gone out of their hopes; a bright light had somehow dimmed. Perhaps, after all, this "pitifully poor little building" was typical of the way everything would turn out. Maybe it wasn't quite as important as they had thought to serve God wholeheartedly. Maybe.

Tainted offer refused

If some of the returnees were happy about rebuilding the temple, and if some were cynical, there was no question how the Samaritans felt. They were determined to stop the construction. Wise in the ways of sin, they figured deception would work better than open confrontation. Their leaders approached Zerubbabel and Jeshua with an offer to help.

"Let us help you build," they said, "because, like you, we seek your God and have been sacrificing to him since the time of Esarhaddon king of Assyria, who brought us here" (Ezra 4:2).

But the returnees were not about to repeat the terrible mistake that Joshua, son of Nun, had made. He had entered into a treaty with one of the local Canaanite tribes even though God had told him not to, and those tribespeople were a thorn in the nation's side ever after (see Joshua 9:1-26). No, Zerubbabel and Jeshua were courteous, but they were also very clear. "Zerubbabel, Jeshua and the rest of the heads of the families of Israel answered, 'You have no part with us in building a temple to our God. We alone will build it for the Lord, the God of Israel, as King Cyrus, the king of Persia, commanded us' " (verse 3).

The rightness of their decision was well proved by what the Samaritans did next. Terrorism is what we would call it today. Ezra described it this way:

> Then the peoples around them set out to discourage the people of Judah and make them afraid to go on building. They hired counselors to work against them and frustrate their plans during the entire reign of Cyrus king of Persia and down to the reign of Darius king of Persia.
>
> At the beginning of the reign of Xerxes, they lodged an accusation against the people of Judah and Jerusalem.
>
> And in the days of Artaxerxes king of Persia ... [they] wrote a letter to Artaxerxes [accusing them of rebellion and sedition] (verses 4-7).

Cyrus's response

Although we know what they wrote in their letter to Artaxerxes, we don't know what they wrote to Cyrus. There's no doubt it was bad, because Daniel tells us how it affected him. He was sick for three weeks.

Cyrus was almost persuaded to side with the Samaritans and tell the returnees to stop building. By this time, Daniel had probably retired. Daniel 1:21 says, "Daniel continued until the first year of King Cyrus" (RSV). The message from the Samaritans arrived in Cyrus's third year. Other advisers were closer to the emperor now, and no doubt many would like to have seen Daniel humiliated. It seems that antisemitism has always been around. Advisers of this type pressured Cyrus to issue a stop order.

So much was at stake! If Jerusalem wasn't rebuilt, there would be no place for Jesus to minister. Then, too, there were Gabriel's assurances that Jerusalem would be rebuilt, based on God's promises. The very honor of heaven was on trial.

Satan knew it. Better than anyone on earth, he realized what was involved. He personally took charge of persuading Cyrus to call a halt.

And Cyrus may well have had second thoughts about his generous decree. Nowhere in history do we read of emperors before him who gave people permission to return to their homeland and, in addition, financed the reconstruction of their chief cities and temples. The Babylonians didn't do it. The Assyrians didn't do it. The Egyptians didn't, nor the Hittites. Historians are probably correct when they say that this magnanimous concept came to Cyrus through reading Isaiah's prophecy under the gentle guidance of Daniel. Cyrus had not limited the gesture to the Jews alone but had sent other captive peoples home with similar financial assistance. Now, so early in his reign, this grand new policy already seemed to be falling apart. His official leaders in Samaria were sending him grave reports of serious misbehavior among people he had trusted.

God dispatched Gabriel to promote heaven's side of the contest. But the battle was too much for him. Jesus Himself became directly involved.

Unaware of the invisible battle, Daniel understood enough about the possible consequences of an unfavorable decision to lose all interest in food. He didn't even wash for "three whole weeks" (Daniel 10:3, KJV), but spent the time in the most intense prayer. His impassioned intercession ended only when Gabriel came and told him the extent to which heaven had been involved in persuading Cyrus to do nothing that would jeopardize the plan of salvation. "The prince of the kingdom of darkness withstood me one and twenty days," Gabriel said. "But, lo, Michael, one of the chief princes, came to help me" (verse 13, KJV).

Cyrus made up his mind on God's side! He let his original decree stand unchanged. The returnees could stay where they were and build the temple.

But the Samaritans went on making life miserable for them. It was a time of testing and, sad to say, the returnees faltered. They stopped building God's house long before it was finished and devoted their time and energy to building their own. Such was the sad, sad effect of the old men's criticism. Was this great new chance headed the way of all its predecessors?

Solving a problem

We'll leave the returnees there for a little while and look at a couple of statements in Ezra 4 that caused me much confusion. They've confused others and may have given you trouble too.

After telling us in chapter 4:5 that the building program was frustrated "down to the reign of Darius king of Persia," Ezra goes on in the next verse to tell us that in the reign of Xerxes a complaint was filed with the king criticizing the Jews. And in the seventh verse he begins a complaint filed with Artaxerxes that resulted in a decree ordering all building activities stopped.

At first reading it seems that these complaints and Artaxerxes's negative decree occur before the second year of Darius, when the building started again. However, historians can't find any Persian kings called Xerxes or Artaxerxes between Cyrus and Darius. The kings they know in that period are called Cambyses and Smerdis. Of course, Xerxes and Artaxerxes might be just different names for these two kings, as some commentators have assumed. But this is highly unlikely, because in all the many written documents that have been discovered referring to Cambyses and Smerdis, they are never called by any name that could be remotely understood as Xerxes and Artaxerxes.[2]

Bible students for many years have tried to explain why, right after Artaxerxes ordered the returnees to stop building, Tatnai, asking to see their building permit, makes no reference to Artaxerxes's decree forbidding any building. That's one problem. Here's another. When Darius makes his decree, during his second year, why does he talk about Cyrus's decree but *make no mention of Artaxerxes's decree?*

How it actually happened

An explanation is crucial to a clear understanding of what really happened, and, fortunately, it's quite simple. We find the account confusing only because we don't know enough about what was going on. It was perfectly clear to Ezra's contemporaries, who lived while these kings were reigning.

Remember that the exiles, empowered by Cyrus's decree, returned to Jerusalem in 536 B.C. Unfortunately, Cyrus's wise and benevolent reign was cut short in 530 B.C. in an otherwise insignificant battle. He was followed by Cambyses, who invaded Egypt and brought it into the Persian Empire. Because the only roads from Persia to Egypt went through Palestine, this campaign must have brought a lot of traffic and confusion to the little company of returnees.

In 522 B.C. Cambyses died and was followed by Smerdis, more widely known as the false Smerdis because he claimed to be the lawful successor to the throne when, in fact, he wasn't. He set out to reverse some of the wise policies set in place by Cyrus. He reigned only six or seven months, but that was long enough for his soldiers to destroy a great many temples around the empire. Very probably, it was under his orders that raiders attacked the unfinished temple in Jerusalem, knocking down such stones as had already been set in place and pulling up the foundation.

Though we regret it, we can understand why many among the returnees began to say, " 'The time has not yet come to rebuild the house of the Lord' " (Haggai 1:2, RSV).

Still in the year 522 B.C., the false Smerdis was stopped short in his illegal career by Darius I, a strong and fair-minded ruler. It took him most of the next two years to straighten out the problems Smerdis had made, but by 520 B.C. he had brought order out of chaos and had the empire running smoothly again.

This, as we will see, is when Haggai, "in the second year of King Darius" (Haggai 1:2), came with his stirring message that got the returnees building the temple again.

So where should we put that forbidding decree of Artaxerxes that Ezra says so much about in Ezra 4? A quick answer is, Many years later. It is a fact that Artaxerxes issued three statements affecting the returnees. The first, as we will see, was that most important one, which he entrusted to Ezra in 457 B.C. The third he gave to Nehemiah in 444 B.C. (To see where those dates come, look again at the last chart in chapter 1.) The decree of Ezra 4, ordering building to stop, was issued between 457 B.C. and 444 B.C. In other words, Artaxerxes told the returnees to go ahead and build up their city; then he told them to stop, and then he told them it was OK to go on, all in the space of thirteen years. Cyrus and Darius would never have blown hot and cold like that. But it was quite typical of Artaxerxes.

Back to the returnees

With those problems straightened out, let's take a quick glance back at the returnees. The wailing and sneering of the old men discouraged them. But Ezra says that the building stopped only "until the second year of the reign of Darius" (Ezra 4:24). The returnees faltered, but they will revive. There is still hope that this glorious new chance will succeed!

---

1. Jeremiah 32:6-15 gives us what some call the best description of the transfer of property available anywhere for that time in history.

2. See the "Additional Note on Chapter 4" in *SDA Bible Commentary,* vol. 3, pp. 347-350.

Ezra 5, 6; Haggai, Zechariah

Chapter 4
Back On Track

Fifteen years went by, years of opposition and increasing discouragement. The happy, hopeful, determined group that returned to Jerusalem in 536 B.C. and that so quickly restored the altar and laid the new temple's foundations had almost lost their vision. The grand new chance God had given His people was derailed in a swamp, as it were, bogged down in gloom.

By the year 520 B.C. the returnees were busy tending their farms and building their homes and desperately trying to make ends meet; for work as hard as they might, they never had enough to pay their bills. A prolonged drought had shriveled the spring grains and the late-summer grapes and had dried up the olive trees and made walking skeletons of the cattle. All that, on top of the depredations of the Samaritans and this shocking attack on the temple foundations by the false Smerdis.

We don't know whether anyone pointed out that the Samaritans would soon have given up their attacks and Smerdis's ruffians would have been unable to penetrate the temple's strong defenses if the returnees had trusted God to protect them and had finished the temple with the same enthusiasm that they started it. " 'The time has not yet come for the Lord's house to be built,' " many people said (Haggai 1:2). They left God's and went to build their own.

Suddenly, Haggai
At this gloomy and apparently hopeless moment, Haggai appeared almost out of nowhere. Within three weeks everything looked brighter and better.

35

Haggai is introduced to the biblical scene with the dramatic impact of Elijah. Undoubtedly he had been born in Babylonia and had come to Jerusalem with the other returnees, but we are not told this. In fact, like Melchizedek (see Hebrews 7:3), we are told nothing of his ancestry or children. Yet his influence had the confident enthusiasm of Caleb. And the amazing results of his brief ministry (it lasted about seventeen weeks) were not exceeded by any other prophet. They were matched only by the astonishing success of Nehemiah. We know that Haggai belongs to this particular time period because, of all Bible writers, he is the most conscientious about dating his visions. Modern historians date his first vision precisely to August 29, 520 B.C. (see *SDA Bible Commentary,* vol. 3, p. 352).

The Bible calls him Haggai the prophet, and that's all we know of his personal life. Just as Elijah is first seen talking to King Ahab about a famine (see 1 Kings 17:1), so in our first glimpse of Haggai we see him talking to Zerubbabel the governor and Joshua[1] the high priest about a famine. And just as Caleb tried to encourage the Israelites to believe that God would help them conquer Canaan in spite of the giants, so Haggai assured the returnees that God would help them build the temple in spite of the Samaritans. Where Caleb failed, Haggai marvelously succeeded. Haggai said to the discouraged leaders:

> This is what the Lord Almighty says, "These people say, 'The time has not yet come for the Lord's house to be built' " (Haggai 1:2).

But God wanted to know:

> "Is it a time for you yourselves to be living in your paneled houses, while this house remains a ruin?" Now this is what the Lord Almighty says, "Give careful thought to your ways. You have planted much, but have harvested little. You eat, but never have enough. You drink, but never have your fill. You put on clothes, but are not warm. You earn wages, only to put them in a purse with holes in it" (verses 4-6).

Zerubbabel and Joshua agreed that everything he said described the situation perfectly. But what should they do about it? Haggai was ready with God's answer:

> This is what the Lord Almighty says: "Give careful thought to your ways. Go up into the mountains and bring down timber and build the house, so that I may take pleasure in it and be honored," says the Lord. "You expected much, but see, it turned out to be little. What you brought home, I blew away. Why?" declares the Lord Almighty. "Because of my house, which remains a ruin, while each of you is busy with his own house. Therefore, because of you the heavens have withheld their dew and the earth its crops. I called for a drought on the fields and the mountains, on the grain, the new wine, the oil and whatever the ground produces, on men and cattle, and on the labor of your hands" (verses 7-11).

"Foolish" prophetic counsel

Let's admit it. The counsel Haggai gave—to go get wood and build the temple—was contrary to all good reason and logic. When your fields don't produce and you need more money, the sensible thing is to plow the fields more carefully and find some way to earn more money. You don't build temples while your land grows weeds.

It reminds me of the advice another prophet, Ellen G. White, gave the leaders of the Pacific Press 2,400 years later under remarkably similar circumstances. It made a particularly strong impression on me because I first heard of it when I was eleven years old and my father had just arrived at Pacific Press from England to edit *Signs of the Times*. The year was 1936. Workers at the Press were still excited about two things: (1) the part they had played in the San Francisco earthquake thirty years before, and (2) the fact that Pacific Press was prospering during the Great Depression because Press leadership had decided to obey Ellen White. That's the way they explained it. I studied the background later and came to appreciate how right those workers were.

For thirty years prior to the earthquake, Pacific Press had been losing money every year till it was (in today's money) $5 million in debt. For twenty of those years Ellen White had been telling the leaders to concentrate their efforts on printing books and magazines for the church and to stop printing checks and history books and tickets for non-Adventist concerns. The leaders loved her, but obviously her advice was foolish. It was this "commercial work" that brought the Press most of its income. The earthquake in April 1906 damaged their building, and a fire three months later totally destroyed it. Only then did the leaders agree to follow her advice. To their astonishment, within the first year they showed a profit, and they continued to have profits year after year. They paid off their total indebtedness in 1929. No wonder the workers were so excited in 1936 when they told me about it.

The returnees respond

How did the returnees respond to Haggai's "foolish" message?

> Then Zerubbabel son of Shealtiel, Joshua son of Jehozadak, the high priest, and the whole remnant of the people obeyed the voice of the Lord their God and the message of the prophet Haggai, because the Lord their God had sent him. . . . Then Haggai, the Lord's messenger, gave this message of the Lord to the people: "I am with you," declares the Lord (verses 12, 13).

Zerubbabel and Joshua must have been thrilled as they listened to Haggai's message. Church members who have never served as a pastor may not realize how important to the success of the church's program is the quiet enthusiasm of even a few church members. How well I remember the help some of the leading members gave me when, at age twenty-five, I was assigned to my first two-church district. In just two years those tiny congregations built a beautiful elementary school on a ten-acre site now worth at least a million dollars. Talking with one of these dear leaders years later, I commented on the support they had given me. She smiled as she said, "We knew you were young, and we decided to make your ministry successful." Bless her! God bless all like her! May their tribe increase!

I think Paul may have felt that way about Lydia. Moses probably felt the same about Caleb. And Zerubbabel and Joshua, I'm sure, jumped up and hugged Haggai. At last, after all the discouraging things everyone else had been saying for so long, here was one man talking courage and success. Thank you, Haggai! Thank you! May there be someone like you in every Seventh-day Adventist congregation around the world. With you, we'll get the gospel message out in no time, and Jesus *will* come soon!

Just three weeks after Haggai talked to Zerubbabel and Joshua, work on the temple started again. The record says that on the twenty-fourth day of the sixth month (September 21, 520 B.C.), "the whole remnant of the people . . . came and began to work on the house of the Lord" (verse 14).

What a workbee that must have been as once again the sound of hammer on wood, of steel clinking against stone, and of busy people in happy conversation announced that God's work was moving forward once more!

Encouraging promises

Less than a month later (on the twentieth day of the seventh month, October 17), God sent another encouraging message. As more of the ground was cleared, the stakes set, and the foundation trenches dug, it was again painfully clear that this temple would be smaller than the first. To head off discouragement, God instructed Haggai to ask the workers, " 'Who of you is left who saw this house in its former glory? How does it look to you now? Does it not seem to you like nothing?' " (Haggai 2:3).

So God had heard the wailing and criticizing! He wanted to help His people see beyond the bricks and stones and mortar to the great purposes He intended to accomplish in this building. Haggai continued with God's message:

> "Now be strong, O Zerubbabel," declares the Lord. "Be strong, O Joshua son of Jehozadak, the high priest. Be strong, all you people of the land," declares the Lord, "and work. For I am with you," declares the Lord Almighty. "This is what I covenanted with you when you came out of Egypt. And my Spirit remains among you. Do not fear" (verses 4, 5).

Mark those words, "When you came out of Egypt." Through all the long centuries of apostasy and idol worship, God had remembered His original covenant. The returnees were His people still.

And then, to this trembling little band of workers, God made a glorious revelation:

> This is what the Lord Almighty says, "In a little while I will once more shake the heavens and the earth, the sea and the dry land. I will shake all nations, and the desired of all nations will come, and I will fill this house with glory," says the Lord Almighty (verses 6, 7).

This little temple would be filled with the glory of the Messiah Himself. What a promise! Surely every effort to build it would be worthwhile! Even Solomon's temple knew no such glory as this!

Another encouraging prophet

Within five or six weeks of that prophecy (during the eighth month) God began sending helpful messages through another prophet, Zechariah. We know a bit more about him. He was the grandson of Iddo, who was one of the Levites who returned under Zerubbabel (see Nehemiah 12:16). If he was born after the group reached Jerusalem in 536 B.C., he was around fifteen when he delivered his first message in 520 B.C. Since no mention is made of his youth, it is more likely that he was older and had been born in Babylonia.

In his first message Zechariah told the people, "This is what the Lord Almighty says: 'Return to me,' declares the Lord Almighty, 'and I will return to you' " (Zechariah 1:3). God was extending His offers of friendship again.

The work of preparing the foundation moved forward rapidly. On the twenty-fourth day of the ninth month (December 18, 520 B.C.), the returnees gathered to celebrate the second laying of the cornerstone. There was no wailing or belittling this time. It appears that Zerubbabel had asked Haggai to deliver the dedication sermon, and God honored the occasion by giving Haggai two important messages. The first was to all the people.

Gazing over that sea of happy faces, Haggai began:

This is what the Lord Almighty says: . . . "Consider how things were before one stone was laid on another in the Lord's temple. When anyone came to a heap of twenty measures, there were only ten. When anyone went to a wine vat to draw fifty measures, there were only twenty. I struck all the work of your hands with blight, mildew and hail, yet you did not turn to me," declares the Lord (Haggai 2:11, 15-17).

Haggai saw heads all over nodding in agreement. The economic recession had been at least that bad; that's why everyone quit working on the temple; there were too many bills to pay. Would it always be that way?

Haggai answered the unspoken question with the message God had given him for this special occasion:

"From this day on, from this twenty-fourth day of the ninth month, give careful thought to the day when the foundation of the Lord's temple was laid. Give careful thought: Is there yet any seed left in the barn? Until now, the vine and the fig tree, the pomegranate and the olive tree have not borne fruit. From this day on . . ." (verses 18, 19).

You can hear Haggai slow his words, pronouncing each so distinctly that no one will miss any part of the marvelous message; you can almost feel the tingle that ran up his spine as he repeated God's wonderful promise: " 'From this day on *I will bless you*' " (verse 19, emphasis supplied)!

Private testimonies

Haggai's other message was a private testimony for Zerubbabel. How well God knows the self-doubt His earthly leaders suffer under the constant criticism of fault-finding church members. Lest Zerubbabel become discouraged, Haggai told him, " 'I will take you, my servant Zerubbabel son of Shealtiel,' declares the Lord, 'and I will make you like my signet ring, for I have chosen you,' declares the Lord Almighty" (verse 23). How kind of God to say that!

Some time later, Zedekiah received a private testimony for the high priest, Joshua, son of Jehozadak. In a vision Zedekiah saw Joshua standing before the angel of the Lord and Satan standing at his right hand to resist him. Zedekiah heard the Lord say to Satan, "The Lord rebuke thee, O Satan; even the Lord that hath chosen Jerusalem rebuke thee: is not this a brand plucked out of the fire?" (Zechariah 3:2, KJV.) There were more gracious, reassuring words, and Joshua must have been most grateful for them. We can be grateful for them too, for they are for us, "upon whom the ends of the world are come" (1 Corinthians 10:11, KJV).

Flattened mountains

Work on the temple progressed smoothly for a while, and the walls began to take shape, but apparently not as quickly as some wished. The belittling spirit revived. It seems that some returnees still sneered at "the day of small things" (Zechariah 4:10). Others questioned whether the building would ever be completed. The first attempt had failed; why not this one also? One major problem, no doubt, was a shortage of money to pay full-time masons and carpenters. The volunteers, no matter how loyal, still had to take care of things at home.

At this time, Zechariah came to Zerubbabel with a message that must have both encouraged and worried him. Zechariah said:

> This is the word of the Lord unto Zerubbabel, saying, Not by might, nor by power, but by my spirit, saith the Lord of hosts. Who art thou, O great mountain? before Zerubbabel thou shalt become a plain. . . . The hands of Zerubbabel have laid the foundation of this house; his hands shall also finish it (Zechariah 4:6-9, KJV).

God understands that people work better when they get a pat on the back. But did some great mountain of difficulty lie ahead? Zerubbabel soon found out.

"Your building permit, please"

Frankly, I like Tatnai. He did his job, he did it courteously, and he proved to be a real help. But I'm sure Zerubbabel saw him at first as a great mountain that was blocking progress.

Tatnai was the official representative of the Persian government for that area. All he did, really, was to ask to see the building permit. He reminds me of the time I put in a lawn-sprinkling system around my new home in Boise, Idaho, soon after Pacific Press moved there. Digging a trench one evening, I was interrupted by a gentleman in a "City of Boise" car asking to see my permit. I told him, truthfully, I'd be happy to get one if he'd tell me where to go. He told me and let me get on with the job. In the next few days I got the permit and posted the receipt the way I'd been told to. When the job was ready for inspection, the same man looked it over carefully, and—I blush to relate!—told me I ought to go into the business because the job was done better than many he inspected. I think of him as an effective official doing his job courteously, my personal Tatnai.

The temple builders told Tatnai they had been given permission to build by Cyrus, and they might have had no trouble at all if they could have shown Tatnai the copy of the decree they had gotten from the great emperor. We must conclude that it had been stolen by one of the raiding parties. Yet this difficulty turned out to the advantage of the builders, because it brought Cyrus's decree to the attention of Darius; if Zerubbabel had been able to produce the decree for Tatnai, Darius might never have heard about it, and the work might have died for lack of funds. God loves to turn our problems into blessings. Tatnai graciously allowed the builders to continue while he checked their story. He wrote to Darius.

Receiving Tatnai's official account, Darius ordered a search to be conducted to find Cyrus's decree. When Darius read it and learned that its generous provisions had not been carried out, he sent Tatnai his own decree vigorously instructing Tatnai to provide both funds for the building and cattle for the sacrificial offerings. Tatnai thereupon hurried to Jerusalem with the good news, no doubt relieved that he had been courteous on his first visit, or he'd surely have had to eat humble pie this time!

On track at last

With means to buy supplies and pay workers, the building proceeded quickly. Critics kept silent now. The mountain had become a plain. The day of small things had proved the beginning of big things. Just four years and three months after work began, the temple was finished. On—or close to—March 12, 515 B.C., the returnees gathered to dedicate their work. It was a happy event. Crops were good again. Bills were paid up. God had told the people what He wanted them to do. They had done it, and He had blessed them as He had promised.

Six weeks later, they gathered for the Passover. We read that

the children of Israel, which were come again out of captivity, and all such as had separated themselves unto them from the filthiness of the heathen of the land, to seek the Lord God of Israel, did eat, and kept the feast of unleavened bread seven days with joy: for the Lord had made them joyful (Ezra 6:21, 22, KJV).

This great new chance God had given His people was back on track again.

---

1. In Ezra and Nehemiah, the high priest's name is spelled Jeshua son of Jozadak. In Haggai, it's Joshua son of Jehozadak. It's the same man.

Ezra 7, 8

Chapter 5
Free at Last

When God opens a door, we had better go through it. It may never open to us again.

As we have seen, God opened a door for the exiles to return to Jerusalem in 536 B.C. The door closed and did not open again until 457 B.C.—almost eighty years later. By reason of their age, if for no other, no one who refused the first opportunity was able to take advantage of the second.

The same thing had happened in the wilderness. After just two years in the desert, God opened the way for Israel to enter the Promised Land. The adults who refused then never went in. Only their children entered with Joshua thirty-eight years later.

As much as a hundred years ago, Ellen White said that Adventists might have been in the kingdom already. Is it possible that way back then, God had arranged affairs in the world in such a way that the grand climax could have come? Then did He pull back because His people were not ready? Is He delaying now, waiting for another generation . . . and another . . . looking for a group willing to do their part in the final events?

We last saw the returnees in 515 B.C. dedicating their new temple and celebrating a happy Passover. The books of Ezra and Nehemiah tell us almost nothing about them after that until Ezra arrives at Jerusalem in 457 B.C. We can assume that the people tended their farms, looked after their flocks, handled their businesses, brought up their children, and paid their taxes relatively peacefully and routinely. Apparently, too, they worked from time to time on Jerusalem's broken-down wall. That they didn't work on it more diligently may have been from lack of interest, but more likely it was from lack of funds. And perhaps the biggest reason was that the strong hand of Darius guaranteed peace throughout the empire and made the city wall unnecessary.

At the seat of empire, Darius provided strong, fair-minded leadership for about thirty-five years. Judea and the returnees prospered, as did other parts of the empire. Unfortunately, during the last portion of his reign, Darius involved his fighting forces in several costly battles with the Greeks. The battle of Marathon (490 B.C.) is a famous Greek victory that occurred at this time. Persian prestige dropped, and taxes throughout the empire—including Judea—went up.

Xerxes and Artaxerxes

Darius was followed by his son Xerxes, known in the King James Version of the Bible as Ahasuerus, who married Esther. Early in his reign, the Samaritans sent him an official complaint against the returnees (see Ezra 4:6). It must have aroused considerable anxiety in Judea, but apparently came to nothing. It may have stimulated increased activity on the wall.

After rejecting Vashti, Xerxes led a major military expedition against the Greeks and lost dismally. (In most modern versions, Ahasuerus is called Xerxes, so I suppose those of us who grew up calling him Ahasuerus will have to adapt! From here on, I'll call him Xerxes.) His forces won at Thermopylae and burned Athens (480 B.C.), but subsequent battles went against them.

Returning to his palace in Susa, Xerxes picked Esther for his wife. Then, needing funds to recoup the cost of his failed campaign, he grasped at Haman's offer of ten thousand talents of silver in return for permission to massacre the Jews. News of the contract certainly reached Jerusalem, and it's not hard to imagine the alarm it stirred up—or the relief that followed when the returnees, thanks to Esther, learned they would be allowed to defend themselves.

Xerxes was murdered in 465 B.C. by a high-ranking official in his government named Artabanus. Artabanus put the blame on one of Xerxes's sons, Darius, who was executed while protesting his innocence. Artabanus then tried to get Megabyzos to help him murder Alexander, another son of Xerxes. Megabyzos exposed the scheme, Artabanus was executed, and Artaxerxes became king.

Artaxerxes proved to be another weakling, an unpredictable, moody person who could thank a man for saving his life and then order him executed. It's no wonder that the fringes of the empire grew restless. Within two years (in 462 B.C.) Egypt exploded in open rebellion. And among the leaders of Beyond the River, the province on the far side of the Euphrates where Judea and Samaria were located, there was talk of secession.

Unrest helps Ezra

As Paul wrote later, God loves to make all things work out for the good of those who love Him (see Romans 8:28). So God used this unrest to make the government of the returnees independent and to complete the fulfillment of His promise "to restore and to build Jerusalem" (Daniel 9:25, KJV). His chief agents would be Ezra and Nehemiah.

Ezra held a high-ranking office in the Persian government. It seems that there were departments overseeing each of the many different peoples subject to the emperor, and that Ezra was in charge of the department that dealt with Jewish affairs. He was the man Artaxerxes would consult when he had any questions about the Jews. This suggests that Artaxerxes had considerable confidence in Ezra and that Ezra was able to get in to speak to him much more readily than an ordinary citizen might. Ezra used this advantage along with much prayer to accomplish his purpose.

Just why Ezra developed such a burden to go to Jerusalem, he does not tell us. Perhaps it was because he was of the priestly line; he could trace his lineage straight back to Aaron. Maybe he began thinking how out of place it was for a priest to be working at a secular job in a pagan king's court.

He seems to have been a natural-born teacher and researcher. He made a detailed study of Israel's history, which wasn't easy to do in those days. He certainly didn't have a Bible like ours. For one thing, at least three books of the Old Testament had not yet been written.[1] Other parts were scattered in various forms: letters, court records, poems, transcripts of sermons, etc. The books of Moses had been gathered and were recognized as inspired, but even copies of this collection were rare, as we can conclude from King Josiah's surprise and concern when a copy of "the book of the law" was discovered in the temple some fifteen years before the exile began (see 2 Kings 22:8).[2] Ezra apparently gathered many of these records and had copies made (see *Prophets and Kings,* p. 609).

In the course of this study, he became acutely aware that the whole experience of the exile had come about because God's people had disobeyed Him. Did the people who had returned to Jerusalem realize this? He must go and tell them! Never again must the Jews be scattered into foreign lands!

He talked to Artaxerxes about his desire to go to Jerusalem and teach the people of Judea to be loyal to the king and to obey the ancient rules of their God. Did he also suggest that if the priests and Levites—the religious leaders—were to be relieved of taxation, they would be more willing to offer sacrifices and prayers in his majesty's behalf? And that if Jerusalem were given more authority for self-rule, its citizens would be less likely to join in the disaffection of other jurisdictions such as, for instance, Samaria? Just what he said, we do not know; but apparently Artaxerxes asked him to draw up a statement that would include whatever it was he wanted, and he would discuss it with his seven cabinet members.

Ezra made good use of the opportunity. Whether he drew up the statement himself or someone else did, the author was fully conversant with Jewish customs and favorable to Jewish wishes.

People, money, sacrifices, taxes, judgment

He started out by writing the statement in the form of a decree, so that, if accepted, it would have full official authority. The first item in the statement was permission for Jews to leave their homes and return to Jerusalem. Then came a promise of silver and gold from the king and authorization to collect funds from anyone willing to give. Third was a directive to purchase, at the king's expense, bullocks, lambs, rams, and flour for sacrifices and to use royal funds to decorate the temple, "for why should there be wrath against the realm of the king and his sons?" (Ezra 7:23, KJV). The fifth provision made it illegal to tax priests and singers and others connected with the temple service. And the final item—if approved—would authorize Ezra to appoint magistrates and judges to administer justice to all the people of Trans-Euphrates—all who know the laws of your God. And you are to teach any who do not know them. Whoever does not obey the law of your God and the law of the king must surely be punished by death, banishment, confiscation of property, or imprisonment (verses 25, 26).

That paragraph, if approved by the king and his Council of Seven, would restore Judea to the status of a self-ruling entity within the empire. It was a lot to ask for, but Ezra was acting out his faith. He believed God would arrange that freedom for His people.

Imagine Ezra's delight to learn that the king and his Council of Seven approved the statement. The king also authorized Ezra to draw up shorter statements to be given to the different officers Ezra would meet along the way, instructing them to help him. Ezra's heart rose in gratitude to God. He felt a great surge of optimism as he set out to gather a band of exiles to return with him. In his zeal we can be sure he expected a huge group to gather on the green fields at the edge of the irrigation canal that flowed to Ahava, the designated meeting place. It was an unexpected opportunity for the exiles, one that had come about entirely as a result of Ezra's prayers, and he hoped many would take advantage of it.

How disappointed he must have been that so few came, only about eight thousand all together (see *SDA Bible Commentary,* vol. 3, p. 375). Not one person among them was a priest or Levite.

No poor ministers

Before we criticize the priests and Levites for not volunteering to return to Jerusalem with Ezra, let's remember that in Persia they could earn a regular living. In Judea they would be dependent for their income on the giving practices of church members, and their standard of living would be horribly unpredictable. We will see later that between Nehemiah's two terms as governor, while he was back at Artaxerxes's palace, tithes and offerings totally dried up, and priests and Levites had to scramble for a living on their small landholdings. God had not intended it to be that way.

We have become so accustomed to seeing ministers underpaid that most of us don't realize that under God's original plan, the income of the priests and Levites would have been as much as five times the national average, maybe more. Let me show you.

All income-earning Jews were to pay one-tenth of their income as tithe, which was to be divided as wages to the priests and Levites. When Moses counted all the men at the foot of Mount Sinai, there were 603,550 (see Numbers 1:46). For simplicity, call that 600,000.

If we averaged all their wages, we would have what I call the "national average wage." The income of the 600,000 men could be called 600,000 "national average wages." When each of these 600,000 contributed one-tenth of their income as tithe, the total tithe would amount to 60,000 national average wages. This amount was to be distributed among the priests and Levites.

Later Moses counted the priests and Levites and got a total of 22,273 (see Numbers 3:43). For simplicity, let's call this twenty thousand. Because sixty thousand is three times as large as twenty thousand, when the total tithe was distributed among the priests and Levites, each priest and Levite would get an amount equal to three national average wages. Apparently God did not intend His ministers to be poor. But there is more.

The 600,000 who were counted were all grown men "twenty years old or more who were able to serve in Israel's army" (Numbers 1:45). But the count of the priests and Levites included boys "a month old or more" (Numbers 3:43). To make the two counts comparable, we should reduce the Levite count by all the boys and youth under twenty. Shall we estimate this as eight thousand of the twenty thousand, leaving us twelve thousand priests and Levites over twenty years of age? If this is fair, then those sixty thousand national average wages were to be distributed among twelve thousand priests and Levites, providing them with incomes five times the national average. And, of course, they were to receive freewill offerings on top of this, making their income, under God's plan, more than five times the national average.

What comes through from this little exercise in arithmetic is that if the Israelites had been faithful in their tithes and offerings, they would have been abundantly blessed (remember what happened when they listened to Haggai), and the priests and Levites would not only have lived comfortably, they would have had abundance to give to the poor and needy. And maybe we wouldn't think it so virtuous to keep ministers poor today.

But considering reality in Ezra's day, it is no wonder that the priests and Levites didn't care to join his returning group.

On to Jerusalem!

Though disappointed to discover there were no priests or Levites with him, Ezra was not discouraged. He asked everyone to be patient while he sent picked men to a nearby Jewish community to persuade as many priests and Levites as possible to join. These emissaries were successful. On their return with the new recruits, Ezra asked the whole company to join him in fasting and prayer that God would bless their journey and protect them from the dangers of the way. He had refused to ask the king to provide armed guards and wanted to be sure no sin in the camp would remove God's protection.

He carefully placed the gold and silver and precious objects the group was taking to Jerusalem in the hands of twelve responsible men and made an exact record of how much each received. He told them they would be expected to take care of the valuable items until they turned them over to the leaders of the temple in Jerusalem.

On the twelfth day of the first month of the Jewish religious year, in the seventh year of Artaxerxes, April 8, 457 B.C., the group set forth. Undoubtedly Ezra carried in his own baggage the group's most important possession, the favorable decree he had received from Artaxerxes.

Walking northwest, west, and south, they followed the ancient trails of the Fertile Crescent around the great desert. God honored Ezra's faith and kept them safe. After a long, hot journey the group arrived unharmed in Jerusalem. The twelve responsible men handed their precious items to the priests, and Ezra revealed to the leaders the contents of Artaxerxes's decree.

Free at last!

With authority to require the keeping of Jewish laws and to punish disobedience by fines and imprisonment, even by the death penalty and banishment from the country; and with authority to convert non-Jews and "naturalize" them into their citizenry, Judea could hold up its head again among the nations of the world.

After years of exile and humiliation, the nation was free at last. To be sure, the returnees still considered themselves slaves (see Nehemiah 9:36), because they still had to pay taxes to Persia and, no doubt, to give their sons as recruits in Persia's armies. But they were free to educate their children in the faith, to worship God according to the dictates of their conscience, and to conduct their daily lives in harmony with their own laws. Actually, with the authority to exact the death penalty, they were more independent than they would be in Christ's day under the Romans.

No doubt about it, God was keeping His promises. He had promised to bring the exiles back, and He had done so. He had promised to help them build the temple, and He had done so. He had promised to reestablish them as an independent civil community, and now He had done this also.

This new chance God had given His people was firmly based on a strong foundation. God was determined to make it succeed. Would His people continue to cooperate? Ezra was here to help them.

---

1. Ezra, Nehemiah, and Malachi for sure. Probably Esther also. And 1 and 2 Chronicles were not put in their present form until he did it.

2. This means that at the age of twenty-six, the king of Israel had not yet read Genesis, Exodus, Leviticus, Numbers, or Deuteronomy. Not even the priests knew there was a copy in the temple. But according to God's original plan, the king should have made his own copy (see Deuteronomy 17:18). Does this ignorance help explain Israel's repeated apostasies?

Chapter 6
Youth-Led Reform

Ezra's arrival in Jerusalem with his eight thousand new settlers must have created enormous excitement, and the public reading of Artaxerxes's decree must have touched off a major celebration.

Ezra did not set himself up as governor of Judea, though he might have. By this time, nearly eighty years after the arrival of the first returnees, Zerubbabel was no doubt dead, and the fact that we aren't told the name of the current ruler suggests he wasn't a major personality. Artaxerxes's decree had given Ezra authority to appoint magistrates and judges to carry out the laws of God and the king. Apparently he was content to appoint the officers and leave enforcement of the laws to them.

Separated from Samaria

The decree expressly stated that the authority of these new officers was to extend to "all who know the laws of your God" (Ezra 7:25). These, of course, would be the Jews living in Judea; it would not include the Samaritans. By the same token, the decree ended any jurisdiction the Samaritans had held over the Jews.

It was a major step forward. Until now, Zerubbabel and the other leaders in Judea had been on about the same level as a board of county commissioners. They could look after building problems and administer the temple, but they did not have judicial or executive authority. Now they did. The Jews in Judea were a nation among the other nations, subject only to the umbrella of the Persian Empire. This is why Artaxerxes's decree is a watershed in Jewish history.

And the fact that Ezra had persuaded the emperor to make such favorable provisions must have given him enormous prestige in Jerusalem. We can be sure that any office he asked for, the citizens would gladly have given him. But he believed God had called him to teach people about Himself. He had come to Jerusalem to teach, and a teacher he would be.

His choice gave him more influence than any political office ever could have, as events were about to demonstrate.

Bad news

Just who gave Ezra the bad news, the Bible doesn't say. It should have been the priests, because it was a religious matter. But they themselves were part of the bad news. So it was a group of leading laymen who approached Ezra several weeks after his arrival. They told him:

> "The people of Israel, including the priests and the Levites, have not kept themselves separate from the neighboring peoples with their detestable practices. . . . They have taken some of their daughters as wives for themselves and their sons, and have mingled the holy race with the peoples around them. And the leaders and officials have led the way in this unfaithfulness" (Ezra 9:1, 2).

If there is one thing the Bible says again and again, it is that those who worship God must not marry those who don't. Paul put it clearly: "Do not be yoked together with unbelievers. For what do righteousness and wickedness have in common? Or what fellowship can light have with darkness?" (2 Corinthians 6:14). Paul, of course, wrote some five hundred years after Ezra. But the people in Ezra's time had abundant evidence to guide them away from intermarriage with unbelievers.

Genesis records that it was after "the sons of God saw the daughters of men that they were fair; and they took them wives of all which they chose," "that the wickedness of man was great in the earth, and . . . every imagination of the thoughts of his heart was only evil continually." And God said, "My spirit shall not always strive with man" and sent the Flood (Genesis 6:2, 5, 3, KJV).

One would think that example would be enough for all time. But for those who needed them, there were others.

The aging Abraham, anxious to get a wife for Isaac before he should die, subjected his chief servant to a solemn oath:

> "I want you to swear by the Lord, the God of heaven and the God of earth, that you will not get a wife for my son from the daughters of the Canaanites, among whom I am living, but will go to my country and my own relatives and get a wife for my son Isaac."
>
> The servant asked him, "What if the woman is unwilling to come back with me to this land? Shall I then take your son back to the country you came from?" "Make sure that you do not take my son back there," Abraham emphatically replied (Genesis 24:3-6).

For men and women who proudly called Abraham their father, *that* experience should have been enough to stop them from ever marrying outsiders. But there were even more examples.

When Jacob fled his home to escape Esau's anger, Isaac minced no words when he bade Jacob goodbye. " 'Thou shalt not take a wife of the daughters of Canaan,' " he said to his frightened son. " 'Arise, go to Padan-aram, to the house of Bethuel thy mother's father; and take thee a wife from thence' " (Genesis 28:1, 2).

To be sure, those who wish to argue in favor of marrying non-Israelites can point to Moses, who willingly married Zipporah, a woman from Midian. But this is not an example of marrying a nonbeliever. Zipporah's father, Jethro, was a worshiper of the true God. In those days before the Aaronic priesthood, he served as a priest to the people he dwelt among. This proves that the prohibition against marrying outside the faith was not a racial taboo, but a religious one. It was all right to marry someone of a different race if he/she worshiped God faithfully.

Ruth and Orpah illustrate this. They were Moabites. But before Naomi's sons married them, Naomi had converted them. Note Ruth's beautiful promise, "Thy people shall be my people, and thy God my God" (Ruth 1:16, KJV).

"Don't tempt My children to stop loving Me"

To me, the most compelling reason for not marrying unbelievers is not a command or example, such as we've looked at, but God's passionate plea to Moses in the mount. God knows better than we do that love cannot be commanded. It must be won by love, heart reaching out to heart and finding acceptance. So listen to that conversation at Sinai.

God has just passed before Moses and made His famous proclamation, so often quoted: " 'The Lord, the Lord, the compassionate and gracious God, slow to anger, abounding in love and faithfulness, maintaining love to thousands, and forgiving wickedness, rebellion and sin' " (Exodus 34:6, 7). Moses bows before Him and pleads, " 'O Lord, if I have found favor in your eyes, . . . then let the Lord go with us. . . . Take us as your inheritance' " (verse 9).

The Lord agrees to do so and promises to do all sorts of wonders in Israel's behalf. Then He closes with a plea that ought to be quoted as widely as the promise about forgiveness. He says to Moses:

> Be careful not to make a treaty with those who live in the land; for when they prostitute themselves to their gods and sacrifice to them, they will invite you and you will eat their sacrifices. And *when you choose some of their daughters as wives for your sons and those daughters prostitute themselves to their gods, they will lead your sons to do the same* (verses 15, 16, emphasis supplied).

At first reading it seems that a jealous, narrow-minded deity resents his people's eating sacrifices offered to other deities. And that, alas, is about all many commentators seem to see. But a parent's heart senses a much deeper meaning, a plea from the great heart of Love that would eventually die in a desperate effort to bring all His children back to Him.

God loves His children and yearns for them to love Him too. He knows that when we marry those who do not worship Him, we will find less and less time to care about Him. In time, we'll stop loving Him. Then, when we are sick, we'll be afraid to call on Him for healing. When we sin, we will feel unworthy to come to Him for pardon. When we are disheartened, we'll go to others for support and sympathy. He wants us, in every case, to come to Him.

Television stations recently showed what happened when social workers, applying the letter of the law, took little children from their foster parents. The TV camera clearly picked up the cries of one two-year-old as his foster mother reluctantly handed him to the worker. "No, Mommy! No, Mommy! No, Mommy!" the child pleaded. And then the camera turned to catch the foster mother bursting into tears. We can understand that.

Then let us understand how God reacts when His children are taken from Him. "Please," He says to parents, to all parents, from Moses' day to ours, "don't let anyone tempt My children to stop loving Me."

Ezra is ashamed

God had given a great new chance to His people, and when Ezra heard that they had taken wives from among the heathen, he was devastated. He tore his clothes and pulled hair from his head and beard, and "sat down appalled" (Ezra 9:3).

He was so visibly agitated that word spread quickly throughout Jerusalem. An unusually large crowd gathered for the evening sacrifice (about 3:00 p.m.), mostly out of curiosity, no doubt. More kept coming.

Their curiosity changed to consternation when they saw how obviously sincere Ezra was. They saw him fall on his knees, spread out his hands to heaven, and cry, " 'O my God, I am too ashamed and disgraced to lift up my face to you, my God, because our sins are higher than our heads and our guilt has reached to the heavens' " (verse 6).

Ezra acknowledged that it was because of Israel's sins that God had allowed disasters to overtake them.

> But now, for a brief moment, the Lord our God has been gracious in leaving us a remnant and giving us a firm place in his sanctuary. . . . Though we are slaves, our God has not deserted us in our bondage. He has shown us kindness in the sight of the kings of Persia. . . .

> But now, O our God, what can we say after this? For we have disregarded the commands you gave through your servants the prophets, when you said: ". . . do not give your daughters in marriage to their sons or take their daughters for your sons. . . ."
>
> What has happened to us is a result of our evil deeds and our great guilt, and yet, our God, you have punished us less than our sins have deserved and have given us a remnant like this. Shall we again break your commands and intermarry with the peoples who commit such detestable practices? Would you not be angry enough with us to destroy us? (verses 8-14).

A long, reverent, soul-searching hush, broken only by the sobs of troubled hearts, lingered over the congregation after Ezra closed with these words, " 'O Lord, God of Israel, you are righteous! We are left this day as a remnant. Here we are before you in our guilt, though because of it not one of us can stand in your presence' " (verse 15).

Young man leads the reform

By this time the once-excited crowd of curious onlookers had become "a large crowd" of serious, repentant sinners reaching out to God for mercy. There was still, after all these eighty years, a deep desire in the hearts of the children and grandchildren of the returnees to make this great new chance work.

And it was one of these young people, whose grandfather was an original returnee (compare Ezra 10:2 with 10:26), who led the response.

Loud enough for all to hear, young Shecaniah—who had not married an unbeliever but whose father had—said to Ezra:

> We have been unfaithful to our God by marrying foreign women from the peoples around us. But in spite of this, there is still hope for Israel. Now let us make a covenant before our God to send away all these women and their children, in accordance with the counsel of my lord and of those who fear the commands of our God. Let

it be done according to the Law. Rise up; this matter is in your hands. We will support you, so take courage and do it (Ezra 10:2-4).

There are people today who tell us we must lower our standards if we hope to keep our youth in the Adventist Church. They show extensive surveys to prove their point. Let those counselors read Ezra 10 and ponder the words of Shecaniah. That young man said, "Keep the standards high!"

I am increasingly convicted that a great many young people who are leaving our church would stay by if our leadership showed more clearly that it really cares about the things we say we believe.

Youth challenge the church. They criticize everything about it. But they criticize their parents too, and their schools, and their country. God made them to do that. A time must come in every person's life when he believes what he believes on the basis of his own experience and not someone else's.

If, under the pressure of that challenge, church leadership caves in and lowers the standards or finds itself unable to explain and defend our beliefs, the youth will turn away in disgust, and who can blame them? But if we who are leaders—parents, teachers, deacons, elders, pastors, conference presidents, General Conference personnel—hold the line, explain and defend the great truths the church has been entrusted with, and demonstrate in our own lives that maintaining God's high standards and obeying all His commands are matters of the greatest personal concern, then the youth will respect us, their own faith will take strength from our faith, and they will commit their lives and their future to the church for now and all eternity.

That's the way it was in Ezra's day. The people saw very clearly that marrying unbelievers was a matter of the greatest personal concern to Ezra, and they agreed to support him in removing the cancer from the body.

Motion, vote, action

After Shecaniah's speech, the record says that Ezra "put the leading priests and Levites and all Israel under oath to do what had been suggested. And they took the oath" (verse 5). If we think of

Shecaniah's speech as a motion, probably coming at the end of a period of discussion, then putting the people to an oath might be considered as taking the vote. Ezra realized that if he was going to make the necessary changes, he would need the people's support. Apparently the vote was unanimous.

By now the day must have been growing dark. It was too late to do more, and, besides, Ezra was still suffering too much distress over the whole affair. He retired to the office of Johanan, who was destined to become high priest after Eliashib, his father, and "mourned because of the transgression" (verse 6, KJV).

But the next day—or, perhaps, the next—Ezra called the city fathers and temple elders together to consider the best way to proceed. It was decided to bring all the men to Jerusalem and lay the problem before them. So a proclamation went out through Jerusalem and Judea ordering all the men to assemble near the temple within three days, on pain of the loss of their property and banishment from the congregation if they failed to appear on time.

Inasmuch as some villages were nearly fifty miles from Jerusalem (see *SDA Bible Commentary,* vol. 3, p. 385), and three days as the Jews counted time may mean only two days in our time, it is obvious that the proclamation demanded instant obedience.

The men obeyed. Leaving their families to care for homes and farms, they headed at once for Jerusalem, wondering, no doubt, what was important enough to require this sudden gathering, and piecing together every strand of rumor they could pick up. Men with foreign wives were, no doubt, worried.

Meeting in the rain

The appointed day was the twentieth of the ninth month, December 7, 457 B.C., deep in the rainy season. Indeed, in a fascinating detail, the Bible tells us that heavy rain fell that morning on the anxious crowd sitting, shivering, in the public square near the temple.

Rain or not, Ezra was all business. " 'You have been unfaithful,' " he said outright. " 'You have married foreign women, adding to Israel's guilt. Now make confession to the Lord, the God of your fathers, and do his will. Separate yourselves from the peoples around you and from your foreign wives' " (verses 10, 11).

No doubt he said more, and what we have is a summary. The people were convinced. As one voice, they responded, " 'You are right! We must do as you say' " (verse 12). But many couples were involved, and the matter could not be finished in a morning. The men asked Ezra to set up a committee to make a thorough investigation and to appoint times when offending couples could come to Jerusalem and present their case. Significantly, the vote was almost unanimous; only four men opposed. They had not married foreign wives and may have opposed, not the action, but the delay in carrying it out.

A committee was appointed and a schedule set up. Investigation began only ten days after the mass meeting—on the first of the tenth month, December 18. Ezra, apparently, was determined to give the problem no time to fester.

The difficult assignment was finished on the first day of the first month, which seems like only three months but was more likely four, since an extra month was probably added during this period to be sure the barley crop would be ripe enough for the wavesheaf offering on the third day after Passover (see *SDA Bible Commentary,* vol. 3, p. 386).

Four months, four weeks to a month, six days to a week—a total of about ninety-six days. Some Bibles list 113 married men; others, only 111.[1] That provides almost a day for each couple. Simpler cases must have been given less time as, perhaps, when there were no children. The offending Israelite was required to confess his sin, make a sin offering, and send away his unbelieving wife and the children. Everyone appears to have cooperated, even the guilty priests.

It's worth trying to analyze why Ezra was so successful. Can we say that the first thing that helped was his own obvious conviction that intermarriage is sinful? I think so. Then he clearly explained his position from the Bible and history. Besides that, he was not afraid to tap the large reservoir of loyalty in the conservative members. Certainly among the most important reasons for his success were that he acted promptly and decisively while the problem was still small. Unfaithful members numbered 113; the faithful numbered over 50,000. He could have said the problem was too small to bother with; he didn't. He rooted out the problem.

What a lot of sad goodbyes there must have been, husbands saying goodbye to their wives, children kissing their fathers for the last time. Tears, loneliness, sorrow. But then, only the devil promised that sin leads to happiness. God never did.

When a person has a malignant tumor, he has to have it cut out or die. The great new chance God had given His people had developed a tumor, and it had to be cut out. Fortunately, the patient cooperated. The prognosis was good.

---

1. The King James Version translates Ezra 10:38, "And Bani, and Binnui," etc., listing both men as unfaithful. The New International Version translates this as "From the descendants of Binnui," following the Greek in the Septuagint and making neither word the name of a transgressor. The Revised Standard Version does almost the same. Possibly, since there were no vowels in written Hebrew in those days, the Septuagint translators treated Bani as *ben,* which means *son.*

Chapter 7
Revenge and Rescue

If William Congreve was right when he said there is no greater fury than a woman scorned, it may be that Ezra's decision to send the unbelieving wives home explains Artaxerxes's unfavorable decree printed in Ezra 4 and helps us determine where to place it in the history of the returned exiles.

When those 113 unconverted women were rejected as unfit to be married to Jewish men, we have to believe that they were very, very angry. And when they reached their pagan homes and told what had happened, whole towns and villages must have exploded in uproar.

Hot heads, we can be sure, called for instant revenge. Cooler heads prevailed. It would not be wise to make an open attack now, not when the emperor's favor was so evidently on the side of Jerusalem.

Memories of insults stretch long, however, and jealousy acknowledges no statute of limitations. Times change. Opportunities return. Revenge might be pushed to the back of the stove for a while, but the stove would be well fed, waiting—

It took about eight, maybe nine years.

Trans-Euphrates rebels

Remember Megabyzos? He's the man who exposed the plot of Artabanus to kill Artaxerxes and seize the throne. You'd think Artaxerxes would have been grateful; if he was, it was hard to tell.

Megabyzos exposed the murder plot in 464 B.C. Two years later, about 462 B.C., Egypt revolted. The need to keep the access roads

open may have been one reason why Artaxerxes made
generous concessions to Ezra in 457 B.C., for Jerusalem was
on the main route. Its continued loyalty was crucial.

Persia's first attempts to quell the uprising failed. Between 456
and 454 B.C. Megabyzos led an army that forced the Egyptians to
their knees. The Egyptian leader, Inarus, begged for terms. Megabyzos promised him, in full faith as a representative of the Persian
emperor, that if he surrendered, his life would be spared.

Inarus surrendered. Egypt was safely back in the Persian fold,
once more part of Artaxerxes's empire, thanks to the faithful,
highly effective Megabyzos.

And a few years later, at his mother's suggestion, Artaxerxes
ordered Inarus murdered.

When the news reached Megabyzos, he was angry, as well he
might be. He was the satrap—or governor—of the province of
Trans-Euphrates. Fed up with the vacillating, unscrupulous ways
of his brother-in-law (he had married Artaxerxes's sister), Megabyzos rebelled, taking Trans-Euphrates with him. The year was
449 or 448 B.C.

Judea was part of Trans-Euphrates. So was Samaria. Eight,
maybe nine years had passed since the wives were sent home.

Revenge!

All these facts are history. Now we must conjecture a little. Do
we have here the setting for that malicious letter the Samaritans
sent to Artaxerxes, accusing the Jews of building the walls to a
rebellious city and urging him to order the work stopped (see Ezra
4:8-16)? I see it fitting in here beautifully. Look at it this way.

The whole province of Trans-Euphrates is in rebellion. Artaxerxes wonders whom he can trust and whom he cannot. It's a
perfect setup for Samaria to win points with the boss by reporting
the disloyalty of a neighboring city.

So the letter is written from

> Rehum the commanding officer and Shimshai the secre-
> tary, together with the rest of their associates. . . . The
> king should know that the Jews who came up to us from
> you have gone to Jerusalem and are rebuilding that

rebellious and wicked city. They are restoring the walls and repairing the foundations. . . . We are sending this message . . . so that a search may be made in the archives of your predecessors. . . . You will find that this city is a rebellious city, troublesome to kings and provinces, a place of rebellion from ancient times. That is why this city was destroyed. . . . If this city is built and its walls are restored, you will be left with nothing in Trans-Euphrates (Ezra 4:9, 12, 14-16).

Surely Artaxerxes was smarter than to believe the Samaritans were all that loyal. Nevertheless, Trans-Euphrates was in rebellion. One didn't dare take chances. Artaxerxes ordered the archives to be searched—and enough incidents of Jewish rebellion were unearthed to fully support the Samaritan charges.

"Stop work!"
Back went an order from Artaxerxes:

To Rehum the commanding officer, Shimshai the secretary and the rest of their associates. . . . Issue an order to these men to stop work, so that this city will not be rebuilt until I so order. Be careful not to neglect this matter. Why let this threat grow, to the detriment of the royal interests? (verses 17, 21, 22).

One's imagination easily pictures the jubilation with which the Samaritans received that letter! Rehum and Shimshai and their associates "went immediately to the Jews in Jerusalem and compelled them by force to stop" (verse 23). And not just to stop. While they were about it, they apparently knocked down sections of the wall and burned several gates. And laughed all the way home.

They had gotten their revenge.

But, as an Israelite king said earlier, "Let not him that girdeth on his harness boast himself as he that putteth it off" (1 Kings 20:11, KJV). The story was not finished yet.

But before we check out what happened next, let's check out that decree from Artaxerxes. Even a superficial look shows it is very different from the one Darius sent Tatnai.

A very different decree

In the first place, it should have been addressed to the satrap of Trans-Euphrates. Rehum and Shimshai were merely local officers, too far down the scale to receive communications from Artaxerxes directly. But the satrap was the rebellious and magnificent Megabyzos. The brothers-in-law were not on speaking terms right then. The fact that the order was sent directly from the emperor to a group of local officers is considered good evidence that all this happened during Megabyzos's rebellion.

Note also the contingency expression: "Issue an order to these men to stop work, so that this city will not be rebuilt *until I so order*" (verse 21, emphasis supplied). That's not the way Darius had written to Tatnai. Said Darius: "I decree that if anyone changes this edict, a beam is to be pulled from his house, and he is to be . . . impaled on it" (Ezra 6:11). That was the usual way Persian emperors wrote decrees.

Clearly, Artaxerxes was uncertain. Maybe, as he dictated the decree, he thought back to the conversations he had had with Ezra about spiritual matters (see *Prophets and Kings,* pp. 607, 608). Maybe, too, he remembered what happened in the empire when his predecessor, Xerxes, had permitted Haman to harass the Jews—and what happened to *them* (Xerxes was murdered, Haman was hanged). Whatever his thoughts, his decree left the way open for reversal.

Nehemiah to the rescue

Nehemiah bursts into the Bible with the announcement that in the twentieth year of Artaxerxes he was living in the citadel of Susa when his brother and some friends arrived from Jerusalem. Inasmuch as by this time Nehemiah was the king's cupbearer, one of the highest of all officials, we can believe he had been in Susa for some time, working his way up. He had been born into a family that had chosen not to return to Jerusalem under Zerubbabel, ninety-two years before. And he himself had chosen not to go with Ezra, only thirteen years before, when—probably—he was old enough to have made his own decision.[1]

But it sometimes happens that when parents grow indifferent to their religious traditions, their children develop a burning passion for them. It seems to have worked this way with Nehemiah.

He was familiar with Ezra's trip. It had been widely publicized in the Jewish community. And, of course, he knew of the favorable decree Artaxerxes had given Ezra. Since that time, travelers from Judea, along with regular reports from the satrap's office for Trans-Euphrates, all indicated that the Jews were working diligently on the Jerusalem wall and making good progress. Along with other Jews in Persia, Nehemiah had let himself believe that the difficult days were over. From now on, Jerusalem would prosper.

After several years had gone by, here came news of Megabyzos's rebellion. What effect had it had on Judea? Then there had been this mud-smearing letter from the Samaritans. All the Jews in Susa knew about it; and about the search the king had ordered; and about the damaging evidence the search had turned up. And then, of course, they knew about Artaxerxes's dreadful decree ordering work to stop. What had the enemies done when that decree reached Samaria?

It was so hard to find out. The distance was great; transportation was slow at best. Megabyzos's rebellion had made it worse. Communication was almost impossible.

Then Artaxerxes made peace with his brother-in-law; he couldn't get along without him. Communication routes returned to normal, but at a maddeningly slow pace for someone as anxious as Nehemiah. By the year 444 B.C., Nehemiah still didn't know what had happened in Jerusalem.

Did his brother, Hanani, go to Jerusalem specifically to learn the facts, so he could tell Nehemiah? We don't know. We don't know for sure whether Hanani was a natural brother or some other relative or simply a fellow Jew; the Hebrew word would allow all three. We do know that Nehemiah questioned him and his fellow travelers "about the Jewish remnant that survived the exile, and also about Jerusalem" (Nehemiah 1:2).

The news they gave him was worse than his worst fears. "Those who survived the exile and are back in the province are in great trouble and disgrace. The wall of Jerusalem is broken down, and its gates have been burned with fire" (verse 3).

Nehemiah prays

Nehemiah sat down and wept. For several days he mourned and fasted . . . and prayed.

Nehemiah tells us in his book that he did a lot of praying. It seems that every time he faced any kind of problem, he prayed. This may be the most significant secret of his remarkable success. We see him praying here; we'll see him praying many more times before he fades from our view, leaving a trail of glory.

This time he prayed for four months. And he found, as a long line of godly people have discovered, that prayer is dangerous. God often uses prayer as a channel to put a person to work. You pray for someone to help a needy person somewhere, and God replies, "I'll help *you* help him. Get up off your knees and start working."

Of course, we don't know how Nehemiah's prayer began. Perhaps, right at the start, he said, "Lord, the Jews in Jerusalem are in trouble. Please open the way for me to get over there and help them." Maybe he prayed like that. But is it likely?

Remember, he had chosen not to go to Jerusalem with Ezra; so it's obvious that at that time he didn't want to get personally involved in Jerusalem's affairs. He had devoted the intervening thirteen years to working his way up the social ladder and expanding his wealth. (Nehemiah 5:14-18 implies he was very rich.) Now he stands at the peak. In a country with only two classes, he is in the upper class, definitely. He ranks among the king's most trusted servants, with direct access to the royal presence. Almost certainly, when he began that four-month prayer, he intended for God to send help through someone else.

But somewhere, at some time, God began to say, "Nehemiah, I want *you* to go." As Nehemiah said later, "God had put [it] in my heart" to help Jerusalem (Nehemiah 2:12). Nehemiah, to his eternal credit, accepted God's call.

Getting the facts

The first thing he did then was to get all the facts he could lay his hands on. He tells us that he "questioned" Hanani and the men who had come with him. We know that later, after one nighttime tour of the wall, he was able to assign more than forty groups of people to work immediately. It is much easier to explain how he could do that if he already knew a great deal about the condition of the wall and its gates and about the people who were living in Judea before he arrived in Jerusalem.

His questioning of Hanani and his friends could have included close details of the wall. "Was it all destroyed?" asks Nehemiah.

"No," says Hanani. "Some parts are badly damaged, other sections not so badly."

"Can you make me a sketch?"

Hanani does his best to draw one, with the friends contributing their memories. Then follow evenings estimating how much work each section will require, how much wood the various gates will need, and where the materials will come from. From appropriate government workers he has no difficulty learning the names of important men he will have to deal with. Perhaps he gets someone to draw up blueprints for the governor's mansion he hopes to occupy; we know he got an estimate of materials the mansion would need.

After four months he felt ready to present his proposal to the king. But first he prayed again, extolling God's greatness, confessing the sins of Israel as if they were his own, recalling to God's remembrance His promises to forgive and restore, then closing with "Give your servant success today by granting him favor in the presence of this man [King Artaxerxes]" (Nehemiah 1:11).

Suddenly scared

Four months of planning and praying would be lost in a moment unless Artaxerxes agreed to help. We can be sure that the same care Nehemiah gave to planning what he would do in Jerusalem he also put into planning how to present his proposal to Artaxerxes.

Did he *deliberately* look sad on that April day in 444 B.C., when spring made the land happy with bird song and flowers? He had never appeared sad in the king's presence in the four months since Hanani arrived, so why today, unless he planned it? The king dined with his wife. The wine was ready. Nehemiah took it in.

Artaxerxes demanded, "Why does your face look so sad when you are not ill? This can be nothing but sadness of heart." Nehemiah was suddenly scared. He wrote later, "I was very much afraid" (Nehemiah 2:2).

Why? we wonder. Perhaps because he saw that he was committed; he would have to go forward and complete his proposal now. If he didn't do his part right, and Artaxerxes refused, all would be lost.

Or perhaps he was afraid because he knew how deadly dangerous Artaxerxes's moods could make him. He knew what he had done to Megabyzos. In spite of the fact that Megabyzos had saved him from murder when he was young and had saved him a second time when he was threatened by a lion, in a fit of bad temper Artaxerxes had ordered Megabyzos killed. Just like that! Fortunately, the order was never carried out, but Nehemiah knew he could easily be treated the same way. No wonder he was scared.

Nehemiah said, "May the king live forever! Why should my face not look sad when the city where my fathers are buried lies in ruins, and its gates have been destroyed by fire" (verse 3).

The value of tact

Every aspiring church officer should study the book of Nehemiah. It is a superb manual on leadership. Our churches would operate far more smoothly and effectively if more of us took lessons from this incredibly successful leader.[2]

Consider his answer. How easily he might have said, "It's that stupid decree you gave Rehum and Shimshai. A man in your position should have known the Samaritans are the real rebels." Every word would have been true, and on the way to his execution, Nehemiah could have boasted that he'd told it to the king "just like it is."

What he actually said was equally true but far more tactful. And it got Nehemiah the response he wanted. For Artaxerxes replied, "What is it you want?" (verse 4).

Nehemiah rocketed a prayer to heaven and then said to the king, "If it please the king and if your servant has found favor in his sight, let him send me to the city in Judah where my fathers are buried so that I can rebuild it" (verse 5).

He hasn't named Jerusalem; in this interview, he never does. It might put Artaxerxes on the defensive, and if possible, that is something Nehemiah wants to avoid at all costs.

Nehemiah's planning and praying are producing results. To Artaxerxes, honoring one's ancestors is a matter of the highest importance. He asks Nehemiah how long he will need to be gone and when he will return.

Nehemiah has his answers ready. He tells the king, and the king nods approval. It all sounds reasonable.

Nehemiah continues: "May I have letters to the governors of Trans-Euphrates, so that they will provide me safe-conduct until I arrive in Judah?" (verse 7). And a letter to Asaph, director of the king's forest, to supply timber for the citadel and the city gates and "the residence I will occupy" (verse 8).

Nehemiah has obviously laid his plans well. And God blesses. Nehemiah says, "The gracious hand of my God was upon me" (verse 8). The king not only grants all he asks but agrees to supply servants and an armed escort.

New excitement in old Jerusalem

And so Nehemiah arrives in Jerusalem. The people wonder who he is and why he's come, but he doesn't tell them. He's not ready yet. For one thing, he needs a rest. For another, he wants to "field check" his plans; do they fit the real situation?

On the third night he gets up, and with a few of the men who came with him, he passes through the Valley Gate and inspects the walls as far as he can go, particularly noting the condition of the wall from gate to gate.

In the morning he announces that he has something to say and invites everyone to come and listen. They hear this stranger say, "You see the trouble *we* are in. . . . Come, let *us* rebuild the wall . . . , and *we* will no longer be in disgrace" (verse 17, emphasis supplied). He doesn't say, "*You* are in trouble, *you* should rebuild the walls." He says "We . . . us . . . we." The crowd likes it.

But some object. "We'll need wood for the gates, and there's no money to buy any."

Nehemiah is ready! "The king has given us all we need."

"But it's a huge job. We've been working for years, and the wall's not done yet."

So Nehemiah told them about the "gracious hand of my God

upon me" and assured them that God would continue to be gracious. He spoke with such enthusiasm and confidence that someone in the crowd responded, "Let's start rebuilding." Soon one after another echoed the words, "Let's start." "We can do it." "God will help us." "What are we waiting for?"

Nehemiah's confident faith in God, expressed in his well-laid plans, lighted a similar faith in the crowd that morning. Soon everyone was voting to repair the wall *now*.

And so began what parents would later tell their children and grandchildren was the happiest, friendliest, and most optimistic period of this great new chance God had given His wayward people.

---

1. This conclusion is based on the historical fact that only thirteen years had gone by (457 B.C. to 444 B.C.). If Nehemiah was too young to make his own choice, he was under twelve years old. This would make him less than twenty-five when the king made him his winetaster and began to trust his life to him, and not more than twenty-five when, loaded with regnal authority, he went to Jerusalem and got the wall built. Since this seems too young to be reasonable, he must have been older than twelve when Ezra made his trip, hence old enough to make his own decision. Reason suggests that by 444 B.C. Nehemiah was in his forties, since he stayed in Jerusalem twelve years this time, returned to Susa, and still had energy enough to make the long journey to Jerusalem again and give vigorous leadership for a second term, of unspecified length.

2. In preparing this volume, I read three books that bring out Nehemiah's leadership qualities. They contain many good ideas, and I recommend them to all who want to improve their leadership skills.

Barber, Cyril J. *Nehemiah and the Dynamics of Effective Leadership.* Neptune, N.J.: Loizeaux Brothers, 1976, 1991.

Boice, James Montgomery. *Nehemiah: Learning to Lead.* Old Tappan, N. J.: Fleming H. Revell Company, 1990.

White, John. *Excellence in Leadership: Reaching Goals With Prayer, Courage, and Determination.* Downers Grove, Ill.: Intervarsity Press, 1986.

Chapter 8
Working Together

We don't know how much time passed between Nehemiah's "God will help us build it!" speech and the day work started on the wall. It wasn't long, for Nehemiah already had a plan that would get everyone involved. And what a good plan it was!

He had divided the job into about forty portions, each the right size for an extended family or a large group of friends to complete. Some portions consisted of one burned gate, others were short lengths of badly damaged wall, while others included longer sections that were in better condition.

The first day must have been an exciting one. Everyone was glad that a job they had put off for so long was being tackled at last. And there was a feeling in the air that *this time* the wall would be finished. Such was the influence of Nehemiah's confident, gracious-hand-of-God-upon-me enthusiasm and his thorough preparation.

On that memorable morning, the high priest, Eliashib, and his fellow priests set a good example for everyone by leading the way to the Sheep Gate and a length of wall beyond it, which they had agreed to repair.

The men of Jericho went to work on the next section.

Zaccur, the son of Imri, built next to them.

And next to them, the sons of Hassenaah rebuilt the Fish Gate.

Meremoth had the next section of wall and next to him, Meshullam . . . and next to him, Zadok . . . and so on, all the way around to the Sheep Gate again.

Every part of the wall was included, and everyone who was

willing to work knew what was expected of him. Herein lies a good lesson for all of us who call for work bees to get jobs done at the church or church school. Too often, when members arrive willing to work, no one tells them what to do. After waiting a while, they go home disgusted, never to come to a work bee again. Nehemiah avoided that problem. He'd gone over his membership list and knew what he wanted each member to do.

Dry dust yields gold

By the way, that job-assignment list in Nehemiah 3 yields rich gold when it's carefully sifted. For one thing, it shows that Nehemiah knew his workers by name; people love to have their leader call them by name.

And the list tells us the wide variety of people who cooperated in the project. There were, as mentioned, many priests. Then there was Uzziel, son of Harhaiah, a goldsmith.

And Hananiah, a perfume maker.

And Shemaiah, the guard at the East Gate.

And Malkijah, another goldsmith.

And Rephaiah, ruler of a half-district of Jerusalem.

Hanun and the residents of Zanoah, who not only rebuilt a gate but also repaired five hundred yards of wall.

Shallun, ruler from Mizpah.

People from all kinds of trades and professions worked happily together. And people who lived in distant towns, who could have said it was none of their responsibility to build a wall for Jerusalem, came and helped.

Not just men worked on the wall. "Shallum son of Hallohesh . . . repaired . . . with the help of his daughters" (Nehemiah 3:12).

Of course, the people named weren't the only ones who worked. They were the leaders. Their families—wives, sons, daughters, uncles, aunts, nephews, nieces, and cousins—worked with them.

And they worked hard, as people do when they have a mind for it, removing the rubble, lifting the heavy stones, mixing the mortar, cutting the beams, drilling holes for the bolts for the hinges, making sure everything was right.

And probably keeping an eye on the group working next to them, being sure they didn't get ahead of them, but dropping everything they were doing to go and help when a rock was too heavy or a stone needed an extra-hard shove.

"The people worked with all their heart," wrote Nehemiah (4:6). Yet apparently some worked even harder than others. The record says that Baruch, son of Zabbai, worked "zealously" (3:20), and three or four groups volunteered for two sections.

Some refused

But not everyone helped. This should be an encouragement to all leaders. Not even Nehemiah was able to persuade *everyone* to cooperate. The men of Tekoah volunteered for two sections, "but their nobles would not put their shoulders to the work" (Nehemiah 3:5). And while people came in from many different towns and villages, many more didn't.

So, did that stop the job?

I vividly remember one day in my very first pastorate when I was working with my two small churches to erect a first-class, modern school building. I had been trying for a week or two to get in to see the conference president and finally got an appointment, only to be told when I reached the conference office that the president was on his way to my district to study a piece of land recommended by a member who didn't like what the rest of the members had voted for. He hoped the president would change things his way. I won't go into details, because I don't want anyone to recognize him. Fortunately, the president didn't like any of the properties that disgruntled member showed him. He cautioned me to be sure a solid majority of the members were behind the project and let me proceed as planned.

In the course of time, a prominent church member graded the building site at his own expense, a contractor agreed to supervise the building at half his usual fee, a great many other church members pitched in for free, and our new school took shape. One Sunday morning when, it seemed, practically all the members came out to put on the siding, that disaffected member turned up, worked about an hour, and left. That was all the time he ever spent on the school. But we got it built.

Did you get that? We got the school built and, let me add, paid for *without him.*

I look back on that experience as one of the most exhilarating of my life. It taught me that church projects are not stopped by people who don't want to help; they are accomplished by the people who do. I am convinced that God's work on earth is going to be finished by those who are willing to cooperate with Him. If any of us choose to sit on the sidelines and criticize, the work will be done anyway, and we'll be losers. As a friend used to say, "The Adventist Church is going through to the kingdom, with me if I'm willing to go with it; but if I'm not, then without me."

As we will see, Nehemiah and the willing workers completed the wall without the "nobles of Tekoah" (see Nehemiah 3:5) or anyone else who didn't want to help.

They even got it finished in spite of people who deliberately tried to stop them.

Opposition from the word go

It seems that whenever someone starts something good, there is always someone else wanting to stop it. This should not surprise us, especially when we begin to do the work of God. We should expect Satan to oppose us and to use human beings as his agents.

Nehemiah didn't have to wait long for his opposition to emerge. It came from a familiar source—Samaria. It seems that Sanballat, ruler of Samaria, and his friend, Tobiah the Ammonite,[1] took a dislike to Nehemiah from the day he first showed them his credentials from Artaxerxes. (Samaria was a few miles north of Jerusalem. Ammon lay across the Jordan.) Nehemiah got the distinct impression that day that "they were very much disturbed that someone had come to promote the welfare of the Israelites" (Nehemiah 2:10).

And when, a few days later, they heard that Nehemiah had persuaded the Israelites to finish the wall, they got together with their ally, Geshem, an important Arab, and the three of them demanded of Nehemiah, "What is this you are doing? . . . Are you rebelling against the king?" (Nehemiah 2:19). I can see them brandishing a copy of that decree Artaxerxes had sent them only a few years earlier authorizing them to stop the Jews from working on the wall. All Judea must have watched with bated breath to see how Nehemiah would respond.

Nehemiah gave a courteous, true, and no-nonsense answer. "The God of heaven will give us success," he said confidently. "But as for you, you have no share in Jerusalem or any claim or historic right to it" (verse 20). In other words, "What we are doing is no business of yours." Sanballat's territory was Samaria. The ruler of Judea was Nehemiah, and Nehemiah had his own decree from Artaxerxes permitting him to build the wall.

Can't you feel the lift Nehemiah's answer gave the Jews! Here was a man who would stand up for them! And because he trusted so much in God, they trusted in Him too.

It was a good thing they did, for the opposition grew worse. Sanballat tried ridicule. Rebuilding had scarcely begun when, in front of his soldiers, he scoffed, "What are those feeble Jews doing? Will they restore their wall? Will they offer sacrifices? Will they finish in a day?" (Nehemiah 4:2).

Tobiah, standing at his side, sneered that if a fox leaned against the wall, it would fall down (see verse 3).

But Nehemiah cheerfully affirmed that God would make the work successful. He believed it—there was no doubt about that. So the workers believed too and got on with the work.

Sooner than anyone expected, the repairs were half-finished. The workers were jubilant.

Then came the rumors!

Prepare for attack!

It seems that rumors of the impending attack were first reported by workers who lived some distance away and commuted to the wall. They told Nehemiah that their enemies were plotting a surprise attack.

It's possible Nehemiah didn't appear to pay much attention at first. But the reports kept coming, till ten people had reported the same threats. "Wherever you turn," they said, "they will attack us" (verse 12).

One thing that made the news so serious was that the original three enemies had now allied themselves with a fourth, the men of Ashdod. To see just how serious this was, we must remember that Samaria was to the north, Ammon was on the east, Arabia wrapped around the south, and the Ashdodites, descendants of the Philistines, lived on the west. The little territory of Judea was now totally surrounded by enemies.

So Nehemiah prayed.

Then he carefully thought about the best course to pursue.

And he acted.

He told the workers to put down their tools and arm themselves with swords, spears, and bows. He made a quick tour of inspection, with a suggestion here and a word of encouragement there. Then he told everyone, "Don't be afraid of them. Remember the Lord, who is great and awesome, and fight for your brothers, your sons and your daughters, your wives and your homes" (verse 14).

When the approaching enemy saw armed guards standing on the walls, they gave up, and the workers went back to building.

On guard

From this point on, Nehemiah realized that armed attacks might come at any moment. He also knew that untrained farmers wielding spears and swords may be more of a danger to themselves than to an enemy. So he made good use of the soldiers who had come with him, posting them at strategic places around the wall. Workers who carried materials were asked to use one hand to carry the load and the other to carry a sword or spear. And all the builders—who would need to use both hands to work—were asked to carry a sword at their side.

The workers who lived outside the city were asked to move in, both for their own safety, no doubt, and also so they would be immediately available in the event of a night attack. A man with a trumpet accompanied Nehemiah wherever he went. If at any time an attack should seem imminent and Nehemiah asked him to sound the alarm, everyone was to come to him at once.

Every daylight minute was made use of, from the first light before dawn till twilight faded after sunset and the stars came out. As for Nehemiah and his brothers and guards, none of them, Nehemiah wrote, "took off our clothes; each had his weapon, even when he went for water" (verse 23).[2]

And the building continued. That's something to notice about Nehemiah. He had a goal, and he was going to reach that goal. He solved every problem in a way that would keep the building progressing.

Trouble from within

The attacks by outside enemies no doubt coalesced the builders into a more effective working force. But now a problem arose from within, with far more serious potential.

Some of the poorer Jews, in order to buy food and pay taxes, were forced to mortgage their farms and vineyards to their wealthier brethren. No longer able to earn money from their land, since they didn't own it anymore, they had sold their sons and daughters into slavery. Meanwhile, the wealthier Jews were charging them exorbitant rates of interest on their loans.

Nehemiah tells us that these victimized "men and their wives raised a great outcry against their Jewish brothers" (Nehemiah 5:1), as well they might, and it's not hard to see that the work on the wall could have stopped right then as the workers polarized into quarreling factions.

How Nehemiah skillfully soothed the troubled waters is the subject of our next chapter. Just remember that the problem arose and was solved *immediately,* when the wall was not quite finished.

"Oh, no!" to Ono

Days later the walls were complete. Only hanging the gates remained when a gracious message came from Sanballat and his friends inviting Nehemiah to a conference of equals "in one of the villages on the plain of Ono" (Nehemiah 6:2), perhaps thirty miles northwest of Jerusalem.

Nehemiah might have felt flattered had he not been so alert. He guessed, rightly, that the schemers meant him harm. He sent messengers to tell them, "I am carrying on a great project and cannot go down" (verse 3). Nehemiah had established his options and saw no reason to change them.

The invitation came three more times, and each time he refused. It was as if he were saying, "Oh, no!" to Ono. When the invitation came a fifth time, there was a nasty difference.

The messenger carried an open letter publicly accusing Nehemiah of repairing the walls so he could set himself up as king. It was similar to the charge these enemies had made at the beginning, and just as dangerous. True, Artaxerxes had made Nehemiah governor, and earlier, he had authorized Ezra to revamp the judicial system. But in between, as we have seen, he had reversed himself completely, ordering the work to stop. Nehemiah knew he could easily reverse himself again.

He also realized that for a messenger, going full speed, to take Sanballat's letter to Artaxerxes and return with Artaxerxes's reply would take at least two months, and he intended to have the gates hung long before that. But he must answer the accusation, or many might believe it. So he prayed, "Now strengthen my hands" (verse 9), categorically rebutted the charge—and kept on building.

"Should such a man as I?"

Then, when so little remained to be done, Nehemiah was given counsel that could have ruined him forever. Shemaiah, son of Delaiah, sent him a message asking him to come visit him, since he was shut up at home. Willing to oblige, Nehemiah went. Shemaiah warned him that he had heard that men were planning to kill him some night soon. He advised, "Let us meet in the house of God, inside the temple, and let us close the temple doors" (verse 10).

Do you think it was kind of Shemaiah to be so solicitous for Nehemiah's welfare? Nehemiah didn't! No true follower of God would advise a layman to go into the temple; only the priests were allowed there. Nehemiah saw at once that this man had been hired to frighten him into committing a sin that would destroy his influence. Firmly he said to Shemaiah, "Should such a man as I flee?" (verse 11, KJV). "Or should one like me go into the temple to save his life? I will not go!" (NIV).

Those words come ringing down the centuries to us today. We are leaders too, whether Sabbath School teachers, deaconesses, elders, pastors, or fathers and mothers, big brothers or sisters. We are all leading someone. Our example is influencing the people around us for better or worse.

When we are tempted to do this or that, let us ask, "Should such a man as I do that? Would it help my class members?" "My life is influencing the youth of our church. Should such a woman as I do *this*?"

Let us apply the question to everything we do. What we propose to do might be all right for others, but would it be all right for such a one as I? It may be true that Christians in other churches do what we are thinking of. I am a Seventh-day Adventist. Should a Seventh-day Adventist do it? Nehemiah's job was to rebuild the wall. Anything that would delay that goal he absolutely refused to do. We have a job too, a twofold goal, to cooperate with God in fully reproducing within our lives the perfect character of Christ and preparing in the world a people ready to meet Jesus when He comes. Should such people as we Adventists, with the goals God has given us, do everything that other people feel free to do? Hear Nehemiah's challenging answer, "I will not."

He got his job done. He got it done fast. Could it be that our job is taking us so long because so many of us are vacillating, comforting ourselves that God will forgive our sins but never getting up and doing what He's told us to do?

The wall finished

The wall was finished. Even Sanballat and Tobiah recognized it as a miracle. All the repairs had been done and the gates hung in fifty-two days. When they heard of it, the "surrounding nations were afraid and lost their self-confidence, because they realized that this work had been done with the help of our God" (verse 16). Even this long after, we are amazed too, and give God glory.

The returnees recognized that God had helped them. He had truly kept His promise to bring the captives home. He had given them, not only another chance, but every possible assistance to make it succeed.

Yet Nehemiah realized that Jerusalem would need more than a wall around it to keep it safe. Inside that wall was sin that must be taken care of if God's blessings were to continue.

---

1. Tobiah's family owned an impressive estate across the Jordan, close to a road going up from Jericho. The ruins of their ancestral castle are pictured in the *SDA Bible Dictionary* under "Tobiah."

2. The King James Version says, "None of us put off our clothes, saving that every one put them off for washing." Hebrew scholars tell us that the last part of this verse, Nehemiah 4:23, is very difficult to translate. For an interesting discussion of the problem, see *SDA Bible Commentary,* vol. 3, pp. 411, 412.

Chapter 9
Why Nehemiah Was Angry

Before going on to what happened next, we will go back a few days to examine more carefully how Nehemiah handled a problem that he says made him very angry.

> The men and their wives raised a great outcry against their Jewish brothers. Some were saying, "We and our sons and daughters are numerous; in order for us to eat and stay alive, we must get grain.". . .
> Others were saying, "We have had to borrow money to pay the king's tax on our fields and vineyards. Although we are of the same flesh and blood as our countrymen and though our sons are as good as theirs, yet we have to subject our sons and daughters to slavery. Some of our daughters have already been enslaved, but we are powerless, because our fields and our vineyards belong to others" (Nehemiah 5:1-5).

Nehemiah tells us, "When I heard their outcry and these charges, I was very angry" (verse 6).

Do you fault him for being angry? If so, should you?

Too often we associate anger with uncontrolled rage. There is no question that uncontrolled rage is wrong. But to get angry is sometimes the only Christ-like way to respond.

Paul said, "Be ye angry, and sin not" (Ephesians 4:26, KJV). Dutifully we try to figure a way to be angry without sinning. But is it possible that we should understand Paul as saying, "Don't sin;

get angry!'"? There are times when it may be sin *not* to be angry.
Jesus got angry. Remember the day He preached in a synagogue
where there was a man with a withered hand? He asked the
congregation, "Is it lawful to do good on the sabbath days, or to do
evil? to save life, or to kill? But they held their peace" (Mark 3:4,
KJV). They held their peace! Imagine it! A man in their church was
desperately crippled, and they did nothing to help him. They were
not disturbed. It didn't matter to them whether he suffered—and
that's where they sinned. A man was in trouble, and they didn't
care. Not so Jesus. He "looked round about on them with anger,
being grieved for the hardness of their hearts, [then] he saith unto
the man, Stretch forth thine hand. And he stretched it out: and his
hand was restored whole as the other" (verse 5).

Jesus' anger was not uncontrolled rage. Anger is an emotion.
Take the *e* from the word *emotion,* and you have *motion.* Our
emotions move us to act. Jesus' anger was a powerful emotion that
moved Him to correct a dreadful evil that Sabbath morning.

So was Nehemiah's anger. Nehemiah was clearly and definitely
under control—and just as clearly and definitely his anger moved
him to correct a serious problem.

The world around us is finally getting angry about battered
wives and abused children, and that's good. And about hungry
people in lands far away, and that's good too. Briefly, I'd like to
mention a problem that occurs in many Adventist church schools.
It may be happening in yours. If so, it needs to be corrected at once.
I refer to Seventh-day Adventist children who cry every school
morning, begging their parents not to force them to go back again
to the Adventist classroom where they know they will be teased and
bullied because their clothes aren't as nice as those of the richer
kids or because their family car is dented or because their dads
aren't big, important people. When that happens, teachers, with
the support of the board and the church membership, need to get
angry enough to teach those teasers that their conduct is totally
un-Christ-like and will not be accepted.

Nehemiah's method

Presented with the problem the poor people brought him,
Nehemiah's first response, as we've seen, was to get good and

angry. Then he pondered the charges in his mind. Nehemiah never flew off the handle. In harmony with his usual custom, he carefully thought through what he was going to do and prayed about it.

One thing he may have observed was that the plaintiffs had gotten into financial difficulties for three different reasons. "One class of people complained of families so large that it was impossible to provide them with food, another of having mortgaged their property because of famine, a third of having to resort to the moneylenders in order to pay their taxes" (*SDA Bible Commentary,* vol. 3, p. 413). Many of them, it seems, had fallen into the hands of usurious creditors; none saw any chance of improving their situation. They hoped Nehemiah would provide relief.

After appraising the problem, Nehemiah talked to the "nobles and officials," apparently privately, as Jesus would later counsel His disciples in Matthew 18. He reminded them that they were "exacting usury from your own countrymen!" (Nehemiah 5:7).

His counseling sessions did not accomplish what he hoped for, which is not surprising, since these rich money grabbers were, after all, the "nobles and officials." They figured that no one was going to tell them what to do. They had enjoyed the fruits of their greed for many years and planned to continue.

Nehemiah doesn't say that these problems had been going on a long time, but everything in the account indicates it. Working on the wall without pay for six weeks might reduce a person's petty cash, but it could not possibly bring on the poverty these people were complaining of. When Nehemiah tells us that "the earlier governors—those preceding me—placed a heavy burden on the people" and that "their assistants also lorded it over the people" (verse 15), we can come to no other conclusion than that the "nobles and officials" were thieves who had operated for many years with the full protection of the highest officers. The poor had complained to them, but the men God appointed to be shepherds had proved to be wolves.

Nehemiah's example

Unsuccessful in the private talks, Nehemiah went to the whole congregation, again anticipating Jesus' counsel, "Tell it to the church" (Matthew 18:17).

At this "large meeting," Nehemiah said, "As far as possible, we have bought back our Jewish brothers who were sold to the Gentiles. Now you are selling your brothers, only for them to be sold back to us!" (Nehemiah 5:7, 8). One stands amazed at this man of action. In only six or seven weeks, in addition to all he had done on the wall and all the outside opposition he had faced, Nehemiah had already set the example of buying back children sold into slavery.

"What you are doing," Nehemiah reminded these rich robbers, "is not right" (verse 9). He appealed to them to remember that they were disgracing Israel in the eyes of their enemies. "Let the exacting of usury stop!" he said. "Give back . . . immediately their fields, vineyards, olive groves and houses, and also the usury you are charging" (verses 10, 11).

With so many people watching, there wasn't much else the moneylenders could do but agree. Nehemiah called forward the priests and "made the nobles and officials take an oath to do what they had promised." Then he shook out the folds of his robe as he said, "In this way may God shake out of his house and possessions every man who does not keep this promise" (verses 12, 13).

So another crisis passed. The people said Amen and praised the Lord. The unscrupulous "nobles and officials" did what they had promised. The workers went back to their jobs on the wall.

Facing up

Let's note that Nehemiah had faced up to the nobles and officials. Almost everyone in Jerusalem was too vulnerable to oppose those powerful men. To do what Nehemiah did, they would have put their jobs, their families' welfare, possibly even their lives at risk.

Nehemiah was a wealthy man. A very wealthy man. What he tells us in verses 14 to 18 suggests that back in Persia he personally owned a large number of high-yield investments, supervised by unusually trustworthy brokers who sent him the dividends regularly. When he came to Jerusalem, he might have cozied up to the nobles and officials and played their game with them. He could have bought large acreages from so many distressed farmers. Instead, he specifically tells us, "We did not acquire any land" (verse 16). Knowing that his financial resources and his friendliness with Artaxerxes made him secure against any harm these men could do him, he chose to oppose them in defense of his vulnerable brothers and sisters.

Sometimes vulnerable, sometimes secure

No doubt all of us are vulnerable in some areas and secure in others. All of us must realize that we'd be utterly foolish to lash out at our employer, or even our foreman, whether he's an Adventist or not. And yet, as we look around, we will find that we are secure in areas where others are vulnerable. Take the children I mentioned in an earlier paragraph. Children being teased at school cannot stand up to their tormentors; they are often afraid to report them. It may even be that the parents of those persecuted children cannot come to their defense, because the parents of the bullies have money or position enough to dominate them. Yet someone must stand up for those children if our schools are to grow and prosper. Should we not study to see whether we are secure in those situations in which others are vulnerable, and look for ways to help them?

This can be risky. I remember the Sabbath morning I followed a certain youth leader to a conferencewide rally. He was driving a red sports car, and as we came off the freeway a police car flagged him over. Indignant at the injustice, I pulled in behind and told the officer my friend didn't deserve a ticket. The officer told me I had been driving too fast and that he was about to give me a ticket too. I had a distinct feeling I shouldn't have stopped.

Then there was the day when a committee, of which I was a member, had to make a very important decision. My wife knew how I felt and what I intended to say. Early that morning she asked me, "Do you want to lose your job?"

I said, "I don't think they'd do that."

I thought I was secure. Well, I said what I felt needed to be said, and in the course of time the committee fulfilled my wife's prediction. That was not the end, however. Eventually the General Conference voted the way my friends and I had thought they should. A great institution was saved to the church, and I consider what the committee did to me and my friends a badge of honor we shall always be proud of.

Standing up for others is risky. But Nehemiah did it. Jesus did it. And we must too, whenever there's a chance it will help.

God's welfare program

If the Jews who returned from the exile had followed God's welfare program, there would have been no complaints for Nehemiah to take care of. God's plan was light years ahead of modern welfare programs if for no other reason than that it provided for the rich to share with the poor, yet required the poor to work for what they got. There were no handouts and no complicated record keeping.

We see parts of the plan working beautifully in the book of Ruth, when bachelor Boaz, rejected as too old by the belles of Bethlehem (see Ruth 3:10) and thoroughly smitten by this lovely widow of a relative's son, instructs his servants to pull out stalks from the sheaves and drop them for Ruth to pick up (see Ruth 2:16).

Years before, Moses had told the Israelites, "When you reap the harvest of your land, do not reap to the very edges of your field or gather the gleanings of your harvest. . . . Leave them for the poor and the alien" (Leviticus 19:9, 10).

A forgotten sheaf was to be left for the poor. "When you are harvesting in your field and you overlook a sheaf, do not go back to get it. Leave it for the alien, the fatherless and the widow, so that the Lord your God may bless you in all the work of your hands" (Deuteronomy 24:19). Similar laws were to apply to the olive crop and the grapes (see verses 20-22).

These provisions must have brought great relief to the poor at harvesttime. But what about in between? Sometimes a poor person would have no recourse but to borrow.

Israelites were instructed to lend to the poor without charging interest. "If one of your countrymen becomes poor and is unable to support himself among you, help him . . . so he can continue to live among you. . . . You must not lend him money at interest or sell him food at a profit. I am the Lord your God" (Leviticus 25:35, 37). (It was all right to charge interest when a person borrowed money to invest for his own benefit. Notice that Jesus criticized the unfaithful servant for not putting his talent into the bank, where it would have earned interest. See Matthew 25:27.)

A poor man's wages were not to be held back by his employer; he was to be paid the evening of the day he worked. Moses said, "Pay him his wages each day before sunset, because he is poor and is counting on it" (Deuteronomy 24:15).

A lender could demand a pledge as surety for the return of a loan, but Moses attached humanitarian restrictions. "Do not take a pair of millstones—not even the upper one—as security for a debt, because that would be taking a man's livelihood as security" (verse 6).

I particularly like this next provision. It preserved the poor man's dignity:

> When you make a loan of any kind to your neighbor, do not go into his house to get what he is offering as a pledge. Stay outside and let the man to whom you are making the loan bring the pledge out to you. If the man is poor, do not go to sleep with his pledge in your possession. Return his cloak to him by sunset so that he may sleep in it. Then he will thank you, and it will be regarded as a righteous act in the sight of the Lord your God (Deuteronomy 24:10-13).

But what could a person do when he had borrowed more than he could ever pay back? He must sell his land. He might even have to sell himself and his children into slavery. God made provision for these problems too. "At the end of every seven years," Moses told the Israelites, "you must cancel debts" (Deuteronomy 15:1). It sounded hard for the creditor, but God promised to make up for any loss.

As for a Jew who sold himself into slavery, Moses said, "In the seventh year you must let him go free. And when you release him, do not send him away empty-handed. Supply him liberally from your flock, your threshing floor and your winepress. Give to him as the Lord your God has blessed you" (Deuteronomy 15:12-14). The property owner who had bought the poor person had gotten his money back in the services he had received, and the poor man now had a chance to start over and do better.

Sold land was to be returned at the Year of Jubilee, which came every fifty years (see Leviticus 25:14-17; 32-38). Without this provision, the farmable land in a country as small as Judea would quickly have passed into the control of a few land barons, as we have seen in many countries much larger.

Good plan gutted by greed

God's welfare plan was so good, poverty should not have been a problem in Israel. Unfortunately, the plan was gutted by greed.

Arguments broke out over the simplest provisions. God said, "Don't reap the very edges." But just how wide was an "edge"? If a farmer farmed several narrow strips, as many did, was he required to leave the edges of each strip? Or could he consider the strips as grouped and leave only the edges of the theoretical group? And when was a sheaf "forgotten"? Maybe his wagon wasn't quite large enough for all his sheaves, and he fully intended in the morning to come back for the last one.

To show how complicated God's simple rules became in the hands of greedy landowners faced by the greedy poor, let me quote a few typical passages from the *Mishnah*. The *Mishnah* is a compilation of Jewish rules and laws, based on the Bible and Jewish tradition, put together by learned Jews prior to about A.D. 200. It is believed to reflect beliefs and practices of Jews over many centuries before that. My copy is over eight hundred pages long.[1] We'll look at a few paragraphs.

> What counts as "Gleanings"? Whatsoever drops down at the moment of reaping. If a reaper reaped an armful or plucked a handful, and a thorn pricked him and [what he held] fell from his hand to the ground, this belongs to the householder. [What falls from] within the hand or the sickle [belongs] to the poor; [what falls from] the back of the hand or the sickle [belongs] to the house-holder. [What falls from] the top of the hand or the sickle, R. Ishmael says: [It belongs] to the poor. R. Akiba says: To the householder (*Mishnah*, p. 14. The brackets [ ] are in the original. "R." is short for Rabbi).

> [What is found in] ant-holes while the corn is still standing, belongs to the householder; after the reapers

[have passed over them], what lies uppermost [in the ant-holes] belongs to the poor, and what is beneath belongs to the householder. R. Meir says: It belongs to the poor in either case, since Gleanings that are in doubt are deemed to be Gleanings (*Mishnah,* pp. 14, 15).

See what the arguments do to the "forgotten sheaf":

[Whether any sheaf at] the ends of rows [may or may not be deemed a Forgotten Sheaf] is proved by a sheaf lying over against it. If the householder laid hold of a sheaf to take it to the city and forgot it, they agree that this may not be deemed a Forgotten Sheaf (*Mishnah,* p. 16).

Two sheaves together may be deemed Forgotten Sheaves; three together may not be deemed Forgotten Sheaves. Two heaps of olives or carobs may be deemed "Forgotten Sheaves"; three may not. Two stalks of flax may be deemed "Forgotten Sheaves"; three may not. Two grapes may count as grape-gleanings; three may not. Two ears of corn may count as Gleanings; three may not. These [rulings] are according to the School of Hillel. Of them all the School of Shammai say: Where there are three they belong to the poor; where there are four they belong to the householder (*Mishnah,* p. 17).

Can't you hear the poor wrangling, "This sheaf is mine; you forgot it!" "We can pick up these stalks; you dropped them!" "We can glean here; it's close to the edge of the field!" And the householders retorting, "That sheaf is mine; I remembered it all the time." "You can't glean so close to the edge; my harvesters haven't had time to cut there yet." Et cetera, et cetera, et cetera.

How about our church?

Before we criticize those Jews, let us look into our own church. Are we involved in internal disputes as potentially ruinous to our spirituality as those that spoiled the Jews' spirituality in Nehemiah's

and where they lived and what they did, with the account of the dedication following immediately afterward (in verse 27), I feel comfortable with the conclusion that the dedication occurred as soon after the twenty-fourth of the seventh month as the time it took the choirs and orchestra to prepare their anthems for the big occasion—maybe less than six weeks after the wall was finished. There really wasn't any delay at all, except that we've come to expect Nehemiah to do everything so fast!

A very special month

I think Nehemiah would have dedicated the wall right away, without waiting even those six weeks, except that the seventh month was very special. I see this as the second reason for delay. Nehemiah did not want anything to distract the people from the rich blessings God made available at that time of year. The tenth day of the seventh month was the Day of Atonement, when every Israelite was obliged to give careful study to his relationship with God. By the end of that day, every sin of the previous year and every fault against a neighbor—provided only that it was confessed before the day closed—was forgiven. Nehemiah didn't want to draw attention away from such a wonderful blessing.

Because the tenth day was so important, God had set aside the first day of the month as an annual sabbath. Trumpets were to be blown drawing attention to the approaching Day of Atonement, and the people were to begin serious preparation for it.

Then, beginning on the fifteenth, the Israelites were to celebrate the Feast of Tabernacles, living in booths for a week in remembrance of the forty years their ancestors lived in tents in the wilderness.

With so much going on that month, Nehemiah wisely chose to add no more.

A need for rededication

The third reason I think Nehemiah waited may have been the most important. He realized that before the people dedicated the wall, they needed to rededicate themselves. A greater builder than he, Solomon, had observed, "Unless the Lord builds the house, its builders labor in vain. Unless the Lord watches over the city, the watchmen stand guard in vain" (Psalm 127:1). The walls David had built and the palaces and temple Solomon built had all crumbled when sin separated Israel from her great Protector.

Nehemiah knew there were reasons why God might yet turn His back on Israel. Those rich officials who had treated their poor brethren and sisters so badly had returned what they had stolen, but most were not repentant, only angry, eager for a chance to get back at Nehemiah. "In those days," Nehemiah tells us, "the nobles of Judah were sending many letters to Tobiah, and replies from Tobiah kept coming to them. . . . They kept reporting to me his good deeds and then telling him what I said. And Tobiah sent letters to intimidate me" (Nehemiah 6:17-19). That root of bitterness must be dug out somehow.

There were other reasons God might withdraw His blessing. Nehemiah saw returnees buying and selling on Sabbath. Some had married their children to unbelievers in spite of Ezra's reforms. Many were neglecting to pay their tithe or give their share to support the temple sacrifices. Heartfelt changes were overdue.

In typical fashion, Nehemiah moved quickly to bring those changes about.

I suppose if Nehemiah had lived in the 1990s, he would have called a committee together and asked them to make up a question-naire. Then he would have commissioned the members to sit at their phones and ask as many Israelites as possible, especially the young and middle-aged, what changes they felt the church should make so they would be comfortable supporting it.

And I wonder what recommendations the committee would have come up with. Maybe, do you suppose, to serve hot chocolate and doughnuts during the morning sacrifice, especially on Sabbaths? Perhaps to import a popular music group from Egypt. Would someone have said, "Kids nowadays really dig that Egyptian music." And might someone else, with a smile, have proposed, "We'd better warn the musicians to adapt their lyrics from the psalms, so we can tell the old folks they're singing Jewish hymns"?

Or copy Aaron, perhaps?

Then again, Nehemiah might have chosen to copy Aaron. Aaron certainly succeeded in getting the people of his day out to church.

There were no empty pews when he was in charge of the service. It's vital to keep in mind that that dance the congregation engaged in so enthusiastically around the golden calf was their way of worshiping the Lord. Aaron told them it was a "festival to the Lord" (Exodus 32:5).

Moses tells us in Exodus 32 that after he had been up in the mountain for nearly six weeks talking with God, the people "gathered around Aaron and said, 'Come, make us gods who will go before us. As for this fellow Moses who brought us up out of Egypt, we don't know what has happened to him' " (verse 1).

Aaron, sensing a chance to usurp the power and popularity he envied Moses for, yielded to the temptation. He asked for the people's jewelry, made the golden calf, and announced, "Tomorrow there will be a festival to the Lord" (verse 5). Next morning, the people were so excited by this new way to worship God, they rose early and came in great numbers. Dutifully they sacrificed the required burnt offerings. Then they sat down to eat and rose up to play. This was real fellowship. Aaron, bless him, certainly understood how to get the people involved. Good old Aaron!

It should be pointed out that the people did not take their clothes off and dance nude, in spite of the fact that the King James Version says, "Moses saw that the people were naked; (for Aaron had made them naked unto their shame among their enemies)" (Exodus 32:25, KJV). They were naked, all right, but in the sense that they had thrown away the Lord's covering that protected them from their enemies. A few days later the Lord told Moses to take the Israelites to the Promised Land, " 'but I will not go with you,' " He said (Exodus 33:3.) It was only Moses' pleas that persuaded God to put up with them any longer.

What Nehemiah actually did

Nehemiah certainly didn't want to conduct services that would remove the Lord's protection. His goal—after building the wall—was to make certain of the Lord's protection.

So he built a large wooden platform and asked Ezra to stand on it and read the Bible out loud.

Just think of that! When Nehemiah wanted to help the people get closer to God, he asked old Ezra to read the Bible to them! He didn't even bring in a youth speaker to hold their attention!

And by noon the people,—men, women, youth, and children,—were repenting and confessing their sins and asking God's forgiveness. They voted to hold a week-long camp meeting and have Ezra read to them every day. They separated themselves from the heathen around them and promised—in writing—to serve and obey God faithfully.

Here was revival and reformation and excited, enthusiastic involvement in their church and all it stood for. It was all the things the Adventist Church needs today. How did it happen?

Let's go back and take a closer look.

Busy days

After the walls were finished and the gates hung, Nehemiah had important organizational work to do. Those gates would have to be opened every morning and closed every evening. He appointed his brother, Hanani, mayor of the city and put Hananiah, "a man of integrity" (Nehemiah 7:2), in charge of the police force. He instructed the two men to select gatekeepers to keep the gates closed in the mornings until the sun was hot and to remain on duty until the gates were closed and barred in the evenings. He requested them also to appoint guards, some to be stationed at posts throughout the city and some to watch near their homes.

Here again we see reasons for Nehemiah's success. Everything he did was well organized, he delegated authority, and he gave clear job descriptions to his workers.

Now, at last, Nehemiah had time to get on with solving a problem that, apparently, he had been praying about for some time without finding a solution. He tells us, "The city was large and spacious, but there were few people in it, and the houses had not yet been rebuilt" (verse 4).

The problem, by its very nature, tells us some interesting things neither Ezra nor Nehemiah has mentioned so far. No one really wanted to live in Jerusalem! Perhaps this is the real reason it took so long to repair the wall! The houses that used to be so comfortable were gone. They were rubble cluttering the streets, overgrown with weeds.

Nehemiah knew that for Israel to have a stable government,

there must be a strong center. As he thought and prayed, he tells us, "My God put it into my heart to assemble the nobles, the officials and the common people" (verse 5) to discuss a plan for populating the capital. When they gathered, he asked them all to register their names; and that seems to be as far as he got before the end of the sixth month. He put his plans aside and entered wholeheartedly into the religious activities of the seventh month.

A festival of trumpets

The morning of the first day of Tishri, the seventh month, dawned clear and calm. Across the hills and valleys floated the sound of trumpets blown by the priests, reminding the people that the Day of Atonement was only ten days away and calling all to assemble beside the temple.

Long before those trumpets blew, the hills and valleys had been alive with people,—men, women, and children, already on their way to Jerusalem. Word had gotten around that Ezra had agreed to read the Bible to them, and no one wanted to miss a word.

The way Nehemiah puts it, "They [all the people] told Ezra the scribe to bring out the Book of the Law of Moses, which the Lord had commanded for Israel" (Nehemiah 8:1). That's truly remarkable, when you think of it. Remember how Ezra had exploded on Jerusalem thirteen years before and ordered everyone who had married an unbeliever to put the spouse away or leave the congregation? Many a minister nowadays trembles to point out sin so clearly, lest he lose his hold on his congregation. Ezra did it, and they loved him. Oh, I can imagine that when the Samaritans sent that letter to Artaxerxes, the one that resulted in the decree that shut down the wall building, there were folk then who grumbled that it wouldn't have happened if Ezra hadn't been so insistent about those mixed marriages. But with the wall finished, no one was listening to the grumblers anymore.

I believe that Ezra was what today we would call a consistent Christian gentleman. And he knew his Bible. How he knew his Bible! Ever since his conversion he had devoted his life to it, gathering manuscripts, arranging them, copying them, studying them till, when he spoke, the Scriptures came alive in the hearts of his hearers.

Are we SDAs afraid of the Bible?

How long has it been since you heard a whole chapter read for a Scripture reading? I admit that I've frequently been asked to choose Scripture readings for church services, and I've always kept them down to a few verses, fearful lest anything longer would lose the congregation's attention.

We love to call ourselves people of the Book, but in this the Episcopalians are ahead of us, for their order of service regularly calls for *two* Scripture readings, one from the Old Testament and another from the New. And I hope I never forget how impressed I was the day I attended Sunday-morning worship in a state-run correctional school for girls in Michigan. Sitting in the back, I marveled as those "naughty, wayward" girls quietly filed into that large room, each one carrying a Bible. But what impressed me even more was watching them respectfully following the printed text as the leader read an *entire chapter* from the New Testament, and it was a long one.

The converting power of the law

By daybreak the people had gathered in a large square near the Water Gate. There were fathers and mothers and children—"all who were able to understand" (verse 2)—and servants too, no doubt, and visitors. What they sat on, we do not know; archaeologists have not discovered any collapsible chairs from this period. Probably, when they sat, they sat on the ground or on the piles of rubble scattered everywhere.

They watched fourteen men climb the steps to the high wooden platform Nehemiah had made for this occasion. Then Ezra, one of the fourteen, stepped to the pulpit and opened his copy of the Book of the Law of Moses. They loved that old man, who was so sincere and genuine, and so concerned about them. As he opened the book, they all stood up. "Ezra praised the Lord, the great God; and all the people lifted their hands and responded, 'Amen! Amen!' Then they bowed down and worshiped the Lord with their faces to the ground" (verse 6).

They listened attentively as Ezra read. Chapter 8:3 says he "read . . . aloud from daybreak till noon." Verse 8 says that thirteen Levites (who were not on the platform) "read from the Book of the

Law of God, making it clear and giving the meaning so that the people could understand what was being read." How to put those statements together is a puzzle that would have given us no trouble at all if we had been there. Since we weren't, we'll have to do our best to find the solution.

Ezra read from daybreak till noon, but maybe not all the time. It's very likely that he read a few chapters, then paused. During those pauses, the thirteen Levites mingled with the crowd, answering questions. Perhaps the large crowd divided into study groups, each with a Levite as its leader.

One problem that we know had to be solved was that the Law was written in Hebrew, but in their everyday conversation these sons and daughters of the exile spoke the Aramaic language their fathers and mothers had learned in Babylon. It was similar to Hebrew, but not the same. For them, the chapters Ezra read would have to be translated before anyone tried explaining what they meant.

God's wish list

What passages of the Law Ezra selected he did not tell us. Many commentators think they were chosen largely from Deuteronomy. Here Moses is talking to the Israelites just before he climbs the mountain to die, while they go on across Jordan into the Promised Land. He reviews with that expectant multitude how the Lord led and protected them through the wilderness, and how often they rebelled. What comes through most eloquently are God's promises—His wish list, if you will let me call it that—the wonderful things God wanted to do for the people who were called by His name. He wanted all the people in other nations, who worshiped idols, to see how much better Israel's God took care of His people than their own gods took care of them.

As the Israelites looked across the Jordan that day, Moses urged them to observe carefully the decrees and laws he had taught them,

> for this will show your wisdom and understanding to the nations, who will hear about all these decrees and say, "Surely this great nation is a wise and understanding people." What other nation is so great as to have their

gods near them the way the Lord our God is near us whenever we pray to him? And what other nation is so great as to have such righteous decrees and laws as this body of laws I am setting before you today? (Deuteronomy 4:6-8).

Clearly God wanted the people who were known by His name to be so prosperous, so healthy and happy, so peaceable and crime-free that representatives from all nations on earth would flock to Jerusalem to ask how they could make their countries like Israel. Thus Israel would rule the world, "the head, not the tail" (Deuteronomy 28:13), not by force of arms, but by the Spirit of God working in their hearts and through their hands.

But what also comes through the pages of Deuteronomy is God's certain knowledge that His people would not carefully observe the decrees and laws Moses taught them, till their sins would block God from blessing them. He would have to make them the tail and not the head (see verse 44) and allow the heathen to triumph over them, scattering them across the world.

And yet He would love them still. Moses assured them that when, in the lands of their dispersion, they remembered what God had taught them, "and when you and your children return to the Lord your God and obey him with all your heart . . . then the Lord your God will restore your fortunes and have compassion on you and gather you again" (Deuteronomy 30:1-3).

As Ezra read such passages that morning, the children of the exile had only to look around to see the truth of Moses' words. The broken buildings, the rubble, the weeds all testified that God's people had let Him down. By their open rebellion they had cut short the blessings their kind and gracious God had wanted so much to bestow, and they wept in sorrow for their sins.

They wept so hard that Nehemiah and Ezra stood up to stop them. "Do not mourn or weep," they said. I see Nehemiah pointing to the newly completed wall as proof that God had taken them back. "Do not grieve," he said, "for the joy of the Lord is your strength" (Nehemiah 8:9, 10). They took his advice and enjoyed a wonderful afternoon.

On to better things

Next morning, the priests and Levites and the heads of families gathered with Ezra to study the Law some more. They discovered instructions to hold the Feast of Tabernacles for a week beginning on the fifteenth of the month. After the Day of Atonement, they went into the countryside and cut branches, brought them back, made booths in the city, and every morning for a week assembled to hear Ezra read more from the Book of the Law.

Two days after the feast they entered into a solemn covenant, which we will look at more carefully in the next chapter.

What a wonderful year was 444 B.C.! The wall was built, and the people got right with God. The evidences that this great new opportunity would succeed had never looked more promising.

Chapter 11
Great Rejoicing in Judea

The autumn of 444 B.C. comes down to us as a time of great happiness in Judea. We saw in the previous chapter how the sorrow for sin that followed the reading of the law on the first morning of the seventh month turned into an afternoon of joy when Ezra and Nehemiah reminded the people that God had accepted their repentance and had forgiven their sins.

The next day, the leaders and the heads of families met with Ezra for more Bible study. As we have noticed before, they discovered that Israel had been commanded to keep the Feast of Tabernacles for a week beginning with the fifteenth day of the seventh month. After the Day of Atonement on the tenth, all these descendants of the returnees went out into the hills and cut tree branches and made shelters for themselves and their families on the roofs and in the courtyards, in the streets and in the open spaces of Jerusalem—even in the courts of the temple, there were so many taking part.

Nehemiah 8:17 comments on that Feast of Tabernacles: "From the days of Joshua son of Nun until that day, the Israelites had not celebrated it like this." Remember that Joshua son of Nun was the man who led Israel across Jordan into the Promised Land, so Nehemiah's comment means that Israel had *never* celebrated the feast as they did in that happy autumn of 444 B.C. Yet it had often been celebrated in the reigns of David and Solomon, and the original returnees celebrated it within a few weeks of their arrival in Jerusalem in 536 B.C. (see 2 Chronicles 8:13; Ezra 3:4). So why does Nehemiah say it had never been celebrated "like this"?

Inasmuch as none of the celebrants in 444 B.C. were present at those earlier feasts, they couldn't make that kind of judgment on the basis of their own experience. I am going to guess they felt this way because they had such a wonderful time all week they couldn't imagine anyone having a better one. And why were they so happy?

For one thing, with the wall built and Nehemiah in charge, no one feared their enemies as the returnees did in 536 B.C. Perhaps even more important, the cohesion of the group must have contributed to their joy. In the days of David and Solomon, the kingdom stretched so far that the Feast of Tabernacles must have attracted huge crowds, so that no one had a chance to get very well acquainted with anyone. But here in Jerusalem in 444 B.C., everyone knew everyone. They had worked together for nearly two months building the wall. They had shared the heart-moving experiences of the Feast of Trumpets. Every day of the feast they gathered together to hear the Bible read and explained to them. There was a feeling of oneness that must have been almost euphoric.

The closeness of small churches

It makes me think of a church that has grown quite large now and owns a beautiful sanctuary nearly paid for and has a conference-appointed pastor. But get close to the charter members who worked so hard to build their lovely church, and you may hear them whisper, "Our early days, when there were just a few of us and we had no pastor and we held prayer meeting in different members' homes because we had no building of our own and nearly everyone came because we realized that the success of our church depended on God and *us*, oh, yes"—and you may detect a sigh—"those were the golden years of our church." I mention this simply because there are a great many small SDA churches, and while I pray you will grow larger, I urge you not to become discouraged. God can come closer to some small churches than ever He can to some larger ones. He certainly came close to that small group of Israelites in 444 B.C. Indeed, that may have been the most important single reason everyone felt so happy.

Ezra read the Bible to them every day, and the Levites explained the meaning. Without question, Ezra read from the five books of

Moses. But there is evidence in Nehemiah 9:7-37 that he also read from Joshua and Judges and 1 and 2 Chronicles. The daily Bible studies began with creation and continued down through Abraham and Moses, the Red Sea and Sinai, the conquest of Canaan, the apostasies and revivals under the Judges, and the repeated rejections of the prophets until God let the people go into exile—and brought them out again.

As the people listened, they felt God drawing very close to them—as we have felt at camp meeting when a saint of God has opened the Scriptures and shown us "wondrous things out of Thy law" (Psalm 119:18, KJV). With John Wesley, we have felt our hearts "strangely warmed." And nothing brings members closer to one another and to God than a well-timed altar call, when with our heads bowed, all plead with God to soften the heart of one and another in the congregation, then (peeking, perhaps?) we see those persons go forward. There's closeness then. There's warmth. There's joy.

We don't know how he worded it, but it's clearly evident that Ezra made an altar call at the end of that Feast of Tabernacles, and the whole body of returnees went forward—leaders, helpers, fathers, mothers, youth, and children. There was joy that day in Jerusalem. So much joy, in fact, that the group agreed to come back two days later, on the twenty-fourth of the month, to seal their dedication with a written pledge.

A binding pledge

This pledge is extremely interesting. It isn't drawn up in vague and general terms. It lists specific commands the Israelites had been violating and promises strict obedience in the future.

First was an all-inclusive pledge to keep all of God's commandments.

Second, a pledge not to marry Israelite children to unbelievers.

Third, a pledge not to buy from any vendor on the Sabbath.

Fourth, a pledge to observe the requirements of the seventh year in canceling debts and letting the land lie fallow.

Fifth, a pledge to care for the temple in several ways:
- to pay a third of a shekel every year for the regular services;
- to bring wood at stated times for the altar;

- to give firstfruits of crops and trees;
- to dedicate firstborn sons and firstborn sheep and cattle;
- to give ground meal, grain, wine, and oil;
- to pay a faithful tithe.

I suppose some today would say this pledge represented salvation by works, but it is certain Nehemiah and Ezra did not so consider it, and I think we'd better accept their opinion. They had seen the dreadful results Israel had suffered as a result of disobedience to God's express commands and were determined such suffering would never be experienced again. Certainly Adventists, of all Christians, should agree with them. We claim to be God's remnant people, those who have the faith of Jesus and "keep the commandments of God" (Revelation 12:17, KJV). If we get to thinking that having the faith of Jesus releases us from the necessity of keeping the commandments, we'll be making the same mistake the Israelites made before Nebuchadnezzar burned their city, when they thought that as long as the sacrifices were offered in the temple, their personal obedience to God's commandments was unnecessary. The books of Ezra and Nehemiah, if they do nothing else, show how wrong that pre-exile view was.

The pledge signed

The day of signing was a solemn one. The Israelites came together fasting and wearing sackcloth on their heads as a sign of their contrition. Again they listened, for half the morning, to the reading of the law, then spent the rest of the morning in public confession and worship. Finally some Levites led them in singing a hymn praising God, the Creator.

Someone, probably Ezra, read the pledge, which began with a review of God's blessings to Israel and Israel's repeated disobedience. Then came the binding words, "In view of all this, we are making a binding agreement, putting it in writing, and our leaders, our Levites and our priests are affixing their seals to it" (Nehemiah 9:38).

First to sign was Nehemiah. You expected him to be first, didn't you, and would have been terribly disappointed if he had held back. Among the priests, who signed next after Nehemiah, Ezra modestly let his name be included within the name of his father,

Seraiah (see Ezra 7:1). Then came the principal Levites and political leaders, eighty-four names in all.

The rest of the people—priests, Levites, gatekeepers, singers, and temple servants, together with their wives and all their sons and daughters who were able to understand—all these now joined the nobles and bound themselves with a curse and an oath to follow the Law of God given through Moses the servant of God and to obey carefully all the commands, regulations, and decrees of the Lord our God.

It was a high point in Israel's history, perhaps the highest they ever reached after the Exile. I'm sure God wishes they had stayed there so He could have blessed them as abundantly as He wanted to.

Time to move on

Nehemiah saw it was time to move forward. Jerusalem was protected now not only by its stone wall, but, with the people once again in harmony with God, it was upheld by the "everlasting arms" (Deuteronomy 33:27). Nehemiah could proceed with his next project, building up the capital city's population. We remember that he had gotten a start on the plan in the last few days of the sixth month. After finishing the wall and before the Feast of Trumpets, he had assembled the nobles, the officials, and the common people and asked them to register by families (see Nehemiah 7:5).

I see him during the seventh month working quietly at home between meetings studying this registration list and comparing it with "the genealogical record of those who had been the first to return" with Zerubbabel (Nehemiah 7:5). I don't think he talked much about his intentions during the meetings so as not to attract attention from the good work Ezra and the Levites were doing. But chapter 11, verse 1 strongly suggests that immediately after the signing of the pledge he jumped into action.

First, he persuaded the leaders of the people to settle in the city. Then he called for volunteers. Apparently quite a few responded, to the applause of others who hoped they wouldn't be asked. We would expect the goldsmiths to want the protection of the city's walls. The perfume makers, merchants, bankers, and innkeepers would prefer the city to the country. Nehemiah had figured that one-tenth of the total population should live in the capital, and he still didn't have enough volunteers. So he subjected the people to casting lots until he reached his goal. Just why he settled on the ratio of 90 percent rural to 10 percent urban he doesn't say. Compare it with the ratio in our country today!

It must have taken several weeks for everyone to move in, perhaps months, since most had to build new homes. But the administrative part had been done, and Nehemiah could move on to his ultimate goal, dedicating the wall. In fact, I'm quite sure that by this time he had already asked Jezrahiah to divide the temple singers into two choirs and prepare anthems for the great day (see Nehemiah 12:42). And surely he had also asked the orchestra director to be ready with stirring music for the same occasion.

Rejoicing heard far away

Always a practical man, Nehemiah probably had a practical reason for dedicating the wall as soon as possible. The day in 457 B.C. when the men stood in the rain listening to Ezra was the twentieth day of the ninth month. This year, 444 B.C., the eighth month had already begun. I'm quite sure Nehemiah didn't want the big celebration ruined by bad weather.

As it turned out by all accounts, dedication day dawned bright and clear. Already, before sunup, people were streaming in from everywhere over the province. Probably a good many had arrived the day before, to sleep on the streets all night as many English still do, to get a good spot on a London sidewalk to watch a royal parade. If Nehemiah set the service for the middle of the month—which would have given the musicians three weeks to prepare after the day of the pledge—there'd be a full moon to help make up for the early sunset and late sunrise.

If you looked closely at the crowd that morning, you could see the men and women who had worked so hard on the wall. They certainly wanted to be there! And their children, too, came to see what all the talk had been about for so long. If you looked over toward the temple, you could see the singers gathering; they seemed to be forming two groups and were practicing different snatches of their anthems. Occasionally the slanting autumn sun

off cymbals, harps, and lyres where the orchestra was
ing, testing their instruments, playing scales and phrases.
By this time, children who had thought they had a good view were
complaining to their dads that now someone was standing in front
of them and they wanted to watch the large number of sheep and
goats and bulls that the priests were struggling to keep in control.

The crowd had grown very large. Many a father was holding his
child on his shoulders. Suddenly a shivering, clashing blast from
the cymbals and a long blaring of trumpets announced that the
dedication service was finally starting.

No doubt Ezra gave the dedicatory sermon. Nehemiah, we can
be sure, thanked the builders for their faithful work and cheered
everyone with reminders of the Lord's blessings. The priests
offered a great many sacrifices. The orchestra played and the
choirs sang. What a joyful noise they made!

Soon Nehemiah asked the people to divide into two large groups.
With Ezra and a choir and trumpeters leading one group and
himself with the other choir and the orchestra leading the other,
the two groups walked to the far end of the city, climbed to the top
of the wall, and walked triumphantly back, Ezra's group going to
the right and Nehemiah's to the left. When they neared the temple,
they descended the stairs into the temple courtyard, where they
sang and applauded, "rejoicing because God had given them great
joy. The women and children also rejoiced. The sound of rejoicing
in Jerusalem could be heard far away" (Nehemiah 12:43).

Twelve successful years

In less than four months, Nehemiah had accomplished his
original goals. The wall was built, the civic government was
running smoothly, Israel's enemies had been routed without a
fight, and the people were pledged to live in harmony with God. He
had proved what many successful schoolteachers have found, that
if they are tough on their children between September and Thanksgiving, they can be angels of light to them the rest of the year, have
their full cooperation, and be loved by all. But if they go easy on the
children those first few weeks, hoping to win their friendship by
allowing them to disobey as they please, then no matter how hard
they crack down the rest of the year, they can never bring those

kids into line, and the kids will hate those teachers forever.

Nehemiah had taken the tough course; risking his personal popularity, he had insisted that everyone, rich as well as poor, bring his or her life into line with God's law. He had won universal respect and love. The next twelve years, while he remained to govern Judea, passed so quietly that the Bible records no problems at all. The temple services continued as Moses had prescribed. The people who had agreed to do so moved into the city and built their homes. Nehemiah finally had a chance to build his own too, though he doesn't mention it.

The twelve years were mostly spent in administration. He tells us that "out of reverence for God," at his own expense he daily fed 150 civic leaders besides official visitors from surrounding nations (see Nehemiah 5:17).

When the twelve years were over, he returned to the court of King Artaxerxes. When he came back to Jerusalem some years later, he found things had deteriorated badly in his absence and moved quickly, in his accustomed manner, to correct them. We'll look at that in our next chapter.

But before we leave the memorable events of 444 B.C., there is a very interesting question to ask.

Was 444 B.C. a seventh year?

There isn't any way to tell for sure. The seventh year was, of course, the year of release, when slaves were to be set free and debts canceled. No one year in either Old Testament or New is ever specifically described as a "seventh year." But if everyone is agreed not to get upset arguing about it, we can look at some interesting evidence that 444 B.C. just may have been a seventh year.

Exhibit number 1 is the fact that Ezra read the Bible every day during the Feast of Tabernacles. In his instructions for the feast, Moses said, "At the end of every seven years, in the year for canceling debts, during the Feast of Tabernacles, when all Israel comes to appear before the Lord your God . . . , you shall read this law before them in their hearing" (Deuteronomy 31:10, 11). Ezra did exactly that this year.

Exhibit number 2 is the "great outcry" (Nehemiah 5:1) the people raised because they had had to sell their children and mortgage their farms. Since buying farms and children was legal, it may be that their *real* complaint, not understood by us and not mentioned in the Bible because it was so well understood by everyone then, was that this was the year for canceling debts, and the rich landowners and money tycoons had not voluntarily canceled them and returned the land and children as they should have. This would also help us understand Nehemiah's success in getting them to agree to do so. They knew they were violating an ancient command.

Exhibit number 3 is all the time the people spent repairing the wall. In the seventh year, the land was not plowed; the people ate what grew naturally (see Leviticus 25:1-7). Forbidden to work their farms, they would have plenty of time to build.

Having given those good arguments, we must recognize that we don't know if 444 B.C. was a seventh year. Let's not fight about it. Remember the man who argued so eloquently that the bus would leave the bus stop at 4:40 and not at 4:20 that everyone agreed he won the argument—but he missed the bus!

More important is to find out what made Nehemiah and Ezra so successful. We're going to look at that in chapter 12. If the Israelites had paid more attention to it themselves, this great new chance the Lord gave them would have succeeded forever.

Chapter 12
Growing With God

When I started this study, I confess I looked at Ezra and Nehemiah as biblical lightweights; important, to be sure, but not overly much so. After spending the time with them it has taken to write this book, my respect for them has grown enormously. It has been especially inspiring to see how they grew as they cooperated with God.

Misdirected priest

Ezra appears on the scene as a misdirected priest. He was well-informed as to his lineage, and several of his relatives still clung to priestly traditions. Some had elected to return to Jerusalem with Zerubbabel, but it is evident that Ezra's immediate family had not.[1] When he was old enough to be offered a position in the Persian government, he accepted it. He was curious about Israel's history and made a hobby of learning all he could about it. In time he became recognized as something of an authority on Jewish affairs, and it is in this capacity that we first see him. Had he been content with that government job, he might have kept it for several years and died in obscurity, just another government clerk, unhonored and unknown.

It may well be that his connection to the priestly line is what first gave him access to the Jews' sacred writings. Somehow he was introduced to them, and it is evident from his own comments that he pursued their study with great zeal. What writings he didn't have, he sought out, gathering scrolls and fragments and arranging them and copying them until no man in his day knew the

Scriptures as he did. He introduces himself to us as "a teacher well versed in the Law of Moses" (Ezra 7:6).

And here, I believe, we have the first secret of his growth and of the great religious changes he brought about among the returned exiles. *He studied the Bible.* Not just a verse here and there. Not just the prescribed passages of the current week's Sabbath School lesson. He went far beyond that, searching the Scriptures until the same thing happened to him that happened to John Wesley on that famous night in a little downstairs room in London. Wesley had studied the Bible all his life, he had preached from it, he had held it up before condemned criminals as the one hope of their salvation; but his own heart was cold. Then that night, as an unlearned deacon read from Luther's commentary on Romans, it suddenly came to Wesley that "God had forgiven *my* sins, *even mine.*" He saw the Bible as God's message to *him,* and he was never the same again.

Something similar, apparently, happened to Ezra. He had been studying the ancient writings as history, to make him better able to answer King Artaxerxes's questions about Jewish affairs. But somewhere that history came alive. It wasn't just a record of the past, it was God's message to Israel, to guide their future. More! *The Bible became God's message to him,* to guide *his* future. That's the second secret of Ezra's phenomenal accomplishments.

He saw the Bible as God pleading with Israel to let Him bless them. God had wanted so much to make Israel the nation all nations looked up to, but He had been forced to scatter them among the heathen, the lowest of all nations, because they had not obeyed Him. Yet His arms of love were stretched out still. He was, even now, willing to fulfill His promises to His people if they would do His will.

Ezra realized that he had never understood the Bible that way before. He reasoned, correctly no doubt, that most other Israelites had never understood it that way either. The conviction fastened upon him that he must teach them. What we see from here on in Ezra's life is his response to that conviction. In other words, *Ezra let his faith control his work.* That, surely, is the third great secret of his success.

Ezra's phenomenal accomplishments

From an easily forgettable bureaucrat in a pagan government, Ezra became a force for God whose accomplishments would endure for time and eternity. I can think of five of them. You may easily think of more.

1. He got a decree from Artaxerxes that set Israel free. Ezra could have been satisfied with this as his major lifetime accomplishment, even if Gabriel had appeared and sent him to the king, or, as with Moses, God had appeared to him in a burning bush and commanded him to go. But nothing like that happened here. Ezra's study of the Scriptures and his frequent prayers led him to see that God wanted something better for His people than what they had, and that Artaxerxes could provide it. Acting on his faith, he asked Artaxerxes for it—and got it. Henceforth, within the Persian Empire, Judea was a self-governing entity. Really, it was a phenomenal accomplishment for a forgettable little bureaucrat. But then, Ezra was fast emerging as an unforgettable giant of faith in action.

2. He led eight thousand people back to Jerusalem. Maybe you say that wasn't anything so great. Zerubbabel took fifty thousand, and Moses led far more. But it occurred to me only a few days ago that Zerubbabel and Moses were fulfilling prophecy. They were carrying out plans God had laid long before, and for which He had made ample provision. Ezra's group was Ezra's idea. There is nowhere in the Bible where God promised a second return for the exiles. Ezra thought this one up and asked God to make it happen; and on Ezra's request, God made it happen. Even when Ezra said he wanted God to keep the travelers safe without armed soldiers, God kept them safe without armed soldiers.

Here was a man who had come to believe that God really did want to save His people. He acted in harmony with his belief, and God supported him. The whole event becomes more astonishing the more you think about it.

3. He cleansed Judea of unbelieving spouses. Maybe you don't think this was so great an accomplishment. But look around in our church today and see how many lifestyle problems no one is even trying to solve. Don't forget, too, that Ezra kept the love and loyalty of the vast majority of the returnees. More than that, it seems that

most of the husbands gave up their unbelieving wives willingly.

Ezra tackled the problem because of his deeply felt conviction that interfaith marriage was totally and absolutely wrong and would bring ruin to God's people. God helped him; apparently God feels the same way. Before he acted, Ezra prayed sincerely about what he was going to do. Here is a secret of his success we've scarcely mentioned so far. *He prayed.* Bowing down before God, again and again he took the sins of Israel on himself and pleaded for forgiveness.

God heard and answered. He obviously respected this man, which is why we do well to respect him too. By rooting out the unbelieving spouses, Ezra preserved the faith of those who remained. They, in turn, passed on their faith to us. Let us be grateful.

4. He led the revival and reformation of the seventh month. You may not share my feeling, but I find it delightful that the people asked Ezra to preach to them on that first day of the seventh month and all through the Feast of Tabernacles, and that they came voluntarily from miles around to listen to him read the Scriptures and explain them every morning. This man had been in Jerusalem now for thirteen years. You'd have thought the people would have grown weary of him and his constant Bible reading, especially when he said everyone had to obey what the Scriptures said. But they loved it, they loved him, and they responded to his preaching with a nationwide reformation that set the tone for Israel for five hundred years. Even to our own day, the Jews are known for their Sabbath keeping, the purity of their race, and their devotion to the teachings of their elders. Ezra had a great deal to do with that.

5. He gathered and arranged much of the Old Testament. Great as were his other accomplishments, this one demands our gratitude above all else. He believed the old writings were so important that he devoted his life to gathering and arranging them for others to study. Again, his faith produced actions that will endure through eternity. Millions of people he never knew owe their salvation to him. What a giant of a man he was!

Nehemiah, another giant

Nehemiah was another forgettable functionary when we meet

him first. Butler to the king of the world's greatest empire and more than comfortably wealthy, he must have been envied by many a less successful aspirant. Refusing to go to Jerusalem with Ezra, he had concentrated on his personal goals and reached them well enough to satisfy even the most ambitious social-climbing over-achiever. But everything he achieved could have crumbled in a moment. It was all tied to the Persian Empire, whose doom Daniel had long ago predicted. Worse still, a flash of anger from his temperamental monarch could have cost him in an instant both fortune and life.

But after he had reached his own goals, *Nehemiah began praying about God's goals,* and that's the ultimate secret to Nehemiah's growth. It is reasonable to suppose that he had prayed many times before; nothing in the story suggests that praying was new to him. We should also believe, I'm sure, that all his great organizational skills, which contributed so much to his worldly success, were present and active before he began praying for the exiles in Jerusalem. But he had used his praying and his skills for himself, to reach his own goals. When he began praying about God's goals, something happened that only God can do.

Just exactly what got him interested in the condition of the people in Jerusalem he doesn't tell us. It seems logical that the report he heard from his brother, Hanani, had much to do with it. Perhaps a latent sympathy for the poor and suffering switched on as he listened. Perhaps there was an inherited loyalty to his Jewishness; suddenly he was embarrassed that his people were so poorly used.

Whatever started him, he began praying for God's people, and soon he found himself praying that *God* might reach *God's* goals for *God's* people. That, in itself, was a major switch, and somewhere about then, God began putting into his mind all sorts of ideas about things he could do to help Him reach those divine goals. *Nehemiah accepted God's assignment.* Add that to the other secrets of his success. The rest, as they say, is history. And what exciting history.

Butler to a king, slave to the King of kings

His faith moved him out of the palace across the barren desert to a broken-down city with half-built walls. It changed him from proud wine-taster to an earthly king to humble slave of the King of all kings. And what an extraordinary slave he was! We see a butler grow into the stature of a world-class leader.

When Nehemiah swung his talents in God's direction, he gave them all to God. We see them in use as he talks to Hanani, his brother. Questions are asked, vital information is gathered, plans are laid, jobs assigned, strategies developed. Special prayers are offered. The king is approached, oh, so tactfully, and needed letters and decrees are willingly given.

Then goodbye to the comfortable palace and off across the sweaty desert to discouraged Jerusalem. An early-morning inspection while others sleep; Nehemiah does nothing without preparation. An enthusiastic speech offering his personal assistance; Nehemiah always takes time to get the people on his side. Then the big job is divided, volunteers are invited, specific jobs are distributed—all Nehemiah's way to get things done.

There's opposition, of course, but he meets it bravely and courteously. The wall is finished, but before he dedicates it, he steps out of the limelight to let another lead a spiritual revival. We find that Nehemiah is particularly interested in proper Sabbath keeping, the faith of new families, tithe paying, and support for those daily acts of faith we call the morning and evening sacrifices. He is acutely aware that God cannot achieve His goals for Israel unless the Israelites live in harmony with Him. Only when the people pledge that harmony does he proceed to organize Jerusalem and dedicate the wall.

Then he settles down to twelve years of peaceful and prosperous leadership, enjoying the well-deserved respect of the people he has done so much for.

Meeting problems of the second term

After twelve years in Jerusalem, Nehemiah fulfilled his promise to Artaxerxes and returned to the emperor's palace. But he left his heart in Jerusalem and came back again after a while for a second term as governor, only to discover on his arrival that apostasy and lawlessness had largely taken over. Ezra, apparently, had died, and without his spiritual influence, evil had enjoyed a field day.[2]

The temple services had stopped, because the priests and Levites were not being paid and had returned to their farms. Men were marrying unbelieving women, and their children were growing up unable to speak the Jews' language or understand the sacred Scriptures. "Men in Judah" were "treading winepresses on the Sabbath and bringing in grain and loading it on donkeys, together with wine, grapes, figs and all other kinds of loads. And they were bringing all this into Jerusalem on the Sabbath." Merchants from Tyre, living in Jerusalem, were "bringing in fish and all kinds of merchandise and selling them in Jerusalem on the Sabbath to the people of Judah" (Nehemiah 13:15, 16).

Most glaring and horrible sin of all, Eliashib the high priest had given Tobiah—the very same Ammonite who had given Nehemiah so much trouble while he was building the wall—he had given him permission to move onto the temple compound, right into the rooms Nehemiah had set aside for storing tithes and offerings! As if that weren't bad enough, he had married his grandson to a daughter of Sanballat, the enemy from Samaria.

Characteristically, Nehemiah moved into action. He threw Tobiah's stuff out of the temple, purified the rooms his presence had desecrated, restocked them with tithes and offerings, and put new men in charge. He reorganized the temple services and made sure everyone was paid his proper wages. And he drove Eliashib's grandson and his unbelieving spouse clear away from Judea. He ordered all the others who had married foreign wives to give them up or leave the country. It was harder this time to get their cooperation, but he didn't give up till the land was cleansed.

He stopped the buying and selling on Sabbath. Significantly, he put his personal servants in charge of the city gates and ordered them to close the gates on Friday evening as the sun was going down—a very good thing for Adventists to do today. As the sun goes down at the beginning and closing of the Sabbath, let us gather our families for worship. The merchants objected at finding the gates closed, but Nehemiah persisted. After a while the people accepted the new way, and it became a way of life for them.

That can be said of many of the changes this intrepid reformer accomplished. Sabbath keeping became a way of life for the descendants of the returnees. So did tithe paying and support for the temple. Marrying unbelievers became almost unknown. The

Jews became known as the people of the Book.

Other giants

There simply isn't time to expand on the other giants in the books of Ezra and Nehemiah: Zerubbabel and Joshua, who led the first group back, and Haggai and Zechariah, who did so much to help get the new temple built. What a great work each one of them did, cooperating with God!

The only shameful record in this story is the life of Eliashib, the man God raised up to be high priest. Even he knew a moment of greatness, when he led the first group to repair the city wall. Beyond that, he comes through as a shrimp among whales, allying himself with Israel's enemies—and for what? For monetary gain, perhaps? Or maybe jealousy, as he saw others take over the leadership he had failed to exert? The Bible doesn't say. When the priests that Nehemiah had expelled from the Jerusalem temple established a rival temple on Mt. Gerizim,[3] Eliashib actually helped them. While others around him worked for God and His glory, he chose to work for himself and the devil. With giants all about him, he chose to be a pygmy.

Their work lives on

But the work of the giants lives on. Some observers will grumble, no doubt, that Sabbath keeping became a form, religious purity became racial pride, tithe paying became a petty nit-picking that "neglected . . . justice, mercy and faithfulness" (Matthew 23:23). True, those faults may be cited.

But let us not fail to notice that when God sent His Son into the world, He was able to find for His mother a faithful young woman with inheritance so pure that everyone acknowledged He was the Son of David. When John called Jesus the Lamb of God, all knew what he meant, because lambs were still being offered on the altar Zerubbabel and Joshua had erected. When Jesus made His grand debut, He made it in the very temple that Haggai and Zechariah had inspired the discouraged returnees to build. When the Holy Spirit filled the hearts of the first Christians, it was inside that same city wall Nehemiah had so effectively repaired. And when Jesus, as a boy, studied the Scriptures in the hills above Nazareth, when on the Day of Pentecost Peter preached Jesus crucified and risen again, when Paul proclaimed that repentant sinners are saved by faith, it was copies of the Scriptures Ezra had gathered that they held in their hands and cited as their supreme authority.

Thanks to these giants, to their devoted Bible study, their hours in prayer, their faith that expressed itself in action, their zeal for God's glory, their profound conviction that what God asked His people to do they must do, and their assurance that God's greatest desire was the success and happiness of His people—thanks to all this, the wonderful second chance God gave the Babylonian exiles produced many of the results God hoped for.

We who live in these last days do well to study their example, for upon us depends the success of the one final chance God is giving the people of earth today.

---

1. Ezra 2:2 says that Seraiah returned with Zerubbabel, and Ezra 7:1 calls Seraiah Ezra's father. But by this time, Seraiah was probably being used as a family name. "Ezra was probably the great-great-grandson of Seraiah. In the language of the Bible writers, every descendant is a 'son,' and every ancestor a 'father.' . . . Ezra probably omits the names of his father, grandfather, and great-grandfather, who were undistinguished, and claims descent from Seraiah, the last high priest to minister in Solomon's Temple (2 Kings 25:18)" (*SDA Bible Commentary,* vol. 3, p. 364).

2. In Nehemiah 13:13, Nehemiah calls Zadok "the scribe," a term he had previously reserved for Ezra.

3. This is the temple Jesus discussed with the woman at the well in John 4:19-24. With its mixed religion, half-pagan, half-Jewish, it was a snare and a problem to both Jews and Samaritans for hundreds of years.

Chapter 13
World's Last Chance

We have seen that God loves to give His people one chance after another. We have examined the chance He gave the returnees after the Babylonian exile, and what they did with it. We know He gave the world another chance in the founding of the Christian church and yet another chance to get everything right in the Reformation of the sixteenth century. But will there always be another chance? Or will a time come when the world will have used up all its chances and God says, "Finished"?

The very first promise in the Bible, given to encourage Adam and Eve on the day they were put out of the garden, stated that at some time the serpent would wound the heel of the woman's Seed and that the Seed would bruise the serpent's head. With Satan dead—as the prophecy predicts—sin would be no more, Eden would be restored, and there would be no more need for second chances.

But nothing in the promise says *when* the Seed's heel would be bruised or the serpent slain.

The sacrifices offered by the patriarchs and priests for four thousand years foreshadowed a day when the Lamb of God would provide forgiveness for sin and an end of sinning. On Mount Moriah, about to offer his own son, Abraham saw clearly that God would provide Himself a Ram for an offering. But again, nothing in these experiences said *when*.

Every year, at the annual cleansing of the sanctuary, all Israel was reminded that some day God would judge the world, finally and irrevocably. All who clung to Jesus on that day would be separated from the record of their sinfulness and never again need another chance. All who clung to their sins that day would be separated from Christ and never have another chance.

So apparently it is true that a day will come when there will be no more chances. But *when?* Could it be now?

The disciples' question

Since the final judgment comes, by its very nature, at the end of the world, the disciples' question is the same as the one we want an answer to. They asked Jesus, "What will be the sign of your coming and of the end of the age?" (Matthew 24:3). Jesus' answer was most interesting. Christians would do well to study it more carefully.

Most of the events modern Christians point to as signs that the end is near aren't really conclusive evidence at all. I refer to earthquakes, wars, famines, and so forth. Jesus listed these and told His disciples, "All these things must come to pass, but the end *is not yet. . . .* These are the *beginning* of sorrows" (Matthew 24:6-8, KJV, emphasis supplied).

I have support for saying this from James White himself, writing in the first volume of *Signs of the Times.* This is what he wrote, January 28, 1875, on the front page of the fourteenth issue of that first volume: "Mark this: Our Lord does not mention wars, famines, pestilences, and earthquakes, as signs of his second advent; but, rather, as events of common occurrence." These disasters will trouble the world till Jesus comes. But they don't tell us *when* He will come.

Even the appalling increase in crime is not a sign of the end. There have always been criminals, disobedient children, and breakers of promises. Paul's warning to Timothy (see 2 Timothy 3:1-5) assures us simply that those who teach that there will be a time of peace before Jesus comes are wrong; there will be law breaking clear to the end.

If pestilence were the major sign of the second coming, Jesus should have come in the fourteenth century, when the Black Plague wiped out multiplied millions in many countries. If it were war, certainly Christ should have come in the seventeenth century, when the Thirty Years War practically depopulated Europe. Clearly, those events were not signs that Christ's return was imminent.

He said He would come after the sun and moon were darkened and the stars fell, but He didn't say when those events would occur. He assured the disciples that the "gospel of the kingdom will be preached in the whole world as a testimony to all nations, and then the end will come" (Matthew 24:14). But even that doesn't say *when* the gospel will be preached.

Jesus never did say when on that Tuesday evening of Passion Week, even though the slaying of God's Ram, the bruising of the Seed's heel, the sacrifice of the Lamb of God was only three days away. But He did not disregard the disciples' question. He told them—and us—where to find the answer. He said, "When you see . . . 'the abomination that causes desolation,' spoken of through the prophet Daniel—*let the reader understand*" (Matthew 24:15, emphasis supplied).

What did Daniel say?

In other words, Jesus said, "Go to Daniel. Study him till you understand; then you'll know when the end will come."

And what did Daniel say? Quoting Gabriel, he wrote that verse we've already looked at several times: "Unto two thousand and three hundred days; then shall the sanctuary be cleansed" (Daniel 8:14, KJV). Then he quoted Gabriel's explanation:

> Seventy weeks are determined upon thy people and upon thy holy city, to finish the transgression, and to make an end of sins, and to make reconciliation for iniquity, and to bring in everlasting righteousness, and to seal up the vision and prophecy, and to anoint the most Holy. Know therefore and understand, that from the going forth of the commandment to restore and to build Jerusalem unto the Messiah the Prince shall be seven weeks, and threescore and two weeks: the street shall be built again, and the wall, even in troublous times. And after threescore and two weeks shall Messiah be cut off, but not for himself. . . . And he shall confirm the covenant with many for one week: and in the midst of the week he shall cause the sacrifice and the oblation to cease (Daniel 9:24-27, KJV).

To put Daniel's prophecy in different words, he said that judgment day would begin 2,300 years after a decree was put into effect to restore and rebuild Jerusalem. The correct interpretation of the prophecy, Gabriel said, would be confirmed by two events: (1) Jesus would begin His public ministry sixty-nine weeks after the decree went into effect, and (2) three and a half years after His ministry began, Jesus would die.

That sounds as if we are getting close to the answer *when* the final events will happen. But to find when judgment day begins, we still need to know when the 2,300 day-years began. When was this decree to restore and rebuild Jerusalem? We know now, don't we, after studying Ezra and Nehemiah? The decree was issued in 457 B.C.

Or was it? Yes, it was.[1] But so much depends on that date being right that every Adventist ought to take a critical look at it, so we're sure we can explain it to others, and so we will realize that we really are living in the days of the world's last chance.

A closer look

We've nearly reached A.D. 2000; we have house payments to make and our families to feed; the world is breaking apart at the seams, with people dying by the millions from famine and disease and ethnic hate; we're scraping the barrel to pay school tuition and trying our best to persuade our kids to focus their lives on Christ. Why worry about when somebody took a letter to Jerusalem 2,450 years ago?

The answer is that it is precisely because the world *is* coming apart at the seams, and no one knows how to sew it together; it is precisely because we are trying to persuade our children to focus their lives on Christ that we need to know that it was 457 B.C.—and not in any other year—when Ezra took Artaxerxes's decree to Jerusalem.

You see, we Adventists believe and teach that the little Baby who was born in Bethlehem and grew up to die on Calvary nearly 2,000 years ago was the Saviour of the world and that He is the same Jesus who is coming soon to put the world to rights again. The date 457 B.C. provides vital evidence in proving that that Baby was our Saviour. It is indispensable in proving that He is coming soon.

It is true that the people of Jesus' day recognized that "no one ever spoke the way this man does" (John 7:46), but that by itself doesn't prove Him to be Christ. There have been many other crowd-pleasing orators in history who have drawn multitudes after them—and wonder workers, too, and men willing to sacrifice their lives for their cause. Some even claimed to be the son of David. But only Jesus of Nazareth began His lifework and finished it at exactly the right number of years after Ezra took Artaxerxes's decree to Jerusalem.

The 2,300-day prophecy expressly states that "from the going forth of the commandment to restore and to build Jerusalem unto the Messiah the Prince shall be seven weeks, and threescore and two weeks" (Daniel 9:25, KJV). Three score is, of course, three times twenty, which is sixty. Sixty plus seven plus two makes sixty-nine, and sixty-nine weeks multiplied by the seven days in each week makes 483 days. Taking each prophetic day for a year means that the real Jesus would appear 483 years after the commandment to restore Jerusalem.

The same prophecy says that Messiah shall be "cut off." He "shall confirm the covenant with many for one week; and in the midst of the week he shall cause the sacrifice and the oblation to cease" (verses 25, 27). The "midst" or middle of the week would be three and a half days from the beginning of the week. In other words, three and a half years after Christ began His ministry He was to be cut off. His death would end the sacrifices and oblations the priests had been offering for so many years.

The Man we call our Saviour began His ministry in the fall of A.D. 27 and died on the cross in the spring of A.D. 31, at which time the veil in the temple was mysteriously torn from top to bottom. The temple services were to be sacred no longer.

From the fall of A.D. 27 to the spring of A.D. 31 happens to be exactly three and a half years! Very interesting—and highly supportive of the argument that Jesus was indeed the promised Messiah. So far, so good. But there's more.

Working back 483 years from A.D. 27 brings us to 457 B.C. If the year when Ezra went to Jerusalem with Artaxerxes's decree was *not* 457 B.C., we may have to look for someone else to be our Saviour. But if Ezra *did* go in 457 B.C., then we have evidence—very remarkable evidence—that He certainly is our Saviour and we don't need to look for anyone else.

So the date is important in helping us identify our Redeemer. It is even more important in establishing our belief that Jesus is coming soon and we are living in the days of the world's last chance.

Is 457 B.C. the right date?

It would be nice to answer that question, "Go look on the calendar." But it's not that easy. Our calendar wasn't developed then. No one dated anything "before Christ" in those days because Christ had not yet been born, and no one knew when He would be.

In ancient times every kingdom had its own way of dating. The most common way was to give the number of years since the present king had come to the throne. Thus Ezra tells us that he received the decree and took it to Jerusalem in "the seventh year of Artaxerxes the king" (Ezra 7:7, KJV).

Unfortunately, different nations used different ways to figure the years of their kings' reigns. Usually a king came to the throne some time after the calendar year began. Some nations counted the part of the year that extended from when the king came to the throne until the next New Year's Day as his first year. Others called this portion of a year his "accession" year and said that his first year did not begin until New Year's Day.

For some kingdoms, New Year came in the spring; for others, it came in the fall. For the Jews, the *religious year* began in the spring with the first month; the *secular year* began in the fall with the seventh month.

And, oh, yes, because almost everyone counted months from new moon to new moon, the years never had exactly 365 1/4 days. They added a full month every two or three years. The Jews always did this between the twelfth month and the first, but other nations were not so consistent.

Is there a way through this maze?

Fortunately, yes. And we don't need to think everything was as complicated as it sounds. After all, we, too, have different years. Our calendar year begins with January, but most fiscal years begin with July. We say we began school when we were six and got married when we were twenty-one and so forth, using the years that began with our birth. In every case, converting to an A.D. date involves some difficulties, but we know enough to do it.

And converting "the seventh year of Alexander" to a B.C. date can be done. In fact, historians have known for hundreds of years that it was 457 B.C. or close to it.

Significant clues for making the conversion came from the Egyptian calendar, which may be described as the most precise and also the most inaccurate of the important ancient calendars. Since before the days of Joseph, the Egyptian calendar had exactly 365 days. In this, it was the most precise. But it made no provision for the extra quarter day a full year needs; there were no leap years. Every four years the calendar got one day ahead of the stars. In 730 years it was a full six months ahead. In 1,460 years it was back in step with the stars, but a full year ahead. In this, it was the most inaccurate. But note that it was *consistent* because nobody added any extra months.

As we've seen, the different nations kept track of time by the reigning years of their current monarch. When the king died, they took note of the number of years he had reigned and started counting again with his successor. After a while, a nation would have a list of its kings with the number of years each reigned. Many of these lists are available today. Nebuchadnezzar appears on the Babylonian king list. Artaxerxes shows up on the Persian list.

Help from Ptolemy

As early as about A.D. 150, the famous Greek-Egyptian astronomer and historian Ptolemy, working in Alexandria, Egypt, gathered lists of kings going back hundreds of years. These included, in succession, Babylonian kings, Persian kings, the Ptolemies who ruled Egypt after Alexander defeated Persia, and the emperors of Rome up to his own time.

It wasn't long before historians observed that by laying the Egyptian calendar beside Ptolemy's Canon, as it is called, they could figure the dates of all those kings as they would be on the Egyptian calendar. And because, as we've seen, the Egyptian calendar is different from ours by only 1/4 day per year, it took only a little adjusting of the Egyptian dates to come up with B.C. dates.

The seventh year of Artaxerxes turned out to be 458/457 B.C. That is, his seventh year began in what we would call 458 B.C. and ended some time in 457 B.C.

Over the past 150 years, hundreds of thousands of dated documents written on clay tablets—letters, receipts, bills—have been discovered, so that it is possible to reconstruct detailed calendars for hundreds of years on both sides of 457 B.C. One of these clay documents describes an eclipse of the sun in Nebuchadnezzar's thirty-seventh year, which puts these dates on a firm basis.

We must admit that 458/457 B.C. is close enough for most purposes. Even if we should count the 2,300 days from 458 B.C., we would be sure that the judgment in heaven has already begun, and it would be a big help in identifying Jesus. But if it could be proved that Ezra took Artaxerxes's decree to Jerusalem in 457 B.C., then we wouldn't be merely *close,* we'd be right on target.

After Ptolemy published his canon, historians, mathematicians, and astronomers continued to study the matter. In A.D. 1650, when Archbishop James Ussher drew up a list of dates for the Catholic Bible, he put the date of Ezra's trip ten years earlier, at 467 B.C., because he assumed, mistakenly, that Artaxerxes had reigned several years with his father. Sir Isaac Newton applied his brilliant mind to the problem, studying the historical evidence available to him, and concluded 457 B.C. was correct. When Bishop William Lloyd introduced Ussher's dates into the King James Version in 1701, he used 457 B.C.

It was this date in the margin of his copy of the King James Version that William Miller relied on to establish the date of 1844 for Jesus' return.

But since about 1890, 457 B.C. has been challenged. Some want to go back to 458 B.C. Others insist Ezra didn't live under Artaxerxes I, but under Artaxerxes II, which would put his trip sixty years later—and, incidentally, move 1844 to 1904.

We don't need to be shaken by these claims. The numerous details of events and places and people named in the books of Ezra and Nehemiah added to the evidence provided by letters that went back and forth between the Jews in Jerusalem. Some Jews living at an Egyptian town called Elephantine, correlated with the evidence of all the dates of those hundreds of thousands of clay tablets, confirm 457 B.C. It is a date firmly anchored in history.

The most important proof is that Jesus ministered during the seventieth week following 457 B.C. The moment when the heel of the Seed was bruised, when God's Ram died, when the Lamb of God was slain was at the Passover, as the evening sacrifice was being offered, in exactly the middle of the seventieth week. Gabriel himself had said that event, coming at that precise moment, would "seal up vision and prophecy" (Daniel 9:24). We won't argue with him.

The somber implications

All this leads to the somber realization that the day of judgment did begin in 1844. The world's last chance is now.

We Adventists, who understand these things better than anyone else and who have been favored with revelations of God above any other group on earth, have very little time left to fulfill God's commission to prepare a people to meet Jesus at His coming.

Whether, like Nehemiah, we are leaders organizing large areas of the work; whether, like Ezra, we are students and teachers; or, like Haggai and Zechariah, we encourage those who carry the heavy responsibilities; whether we are masons shoving stones into place or woodsmen supplying fuel for the temple services, let it be said of us as it was said of the returnees, that we worked with all our heart. May it be that because of our contribution, this last chance will end in glory. As a result of our efforts may many from all walks and conditions of life be welcomed into that eternal city, with its alabaster walls and pearly gates, where Jesus Christ will reign as Governor and King for ever and ever more.

---

1. See *SDA Bible Commentary,* vol. 3, p. 365. The ultimate book for establishing the accuracy of the date 457 B.C. is Siegfried H. Horn and Lynn H. Wood, *The Chronology of Ezra 7,* second edition, revised (Washington, D.C.: Review and Herald Publishing Association, 1953, 1970). A concise study of the evidence can be found in *SDA Bible Dictionary,* p. 215 (1979 edition). Other articles that help explain Bible chronology appear throughout the *SDA Bible Commentary.*